RECIPES FROM THE
KITCHEN DRAWER

RECIPES FROM THE KITCHEN DRAWER

a graphic cookbook
by HELEN ASHLEY

to A

introduction

Many of the recipes in this book were inspired by meals from my childhood. Both of my parents were keen cooks, encouraging me to experiment in the kitchen and to eat adventurously from an early age. Thanks to them, too, I grew up surrounded by finely illustrated recipe books: Elizabeth David's *A Book of Mediterranean Food*, with drawings by John Minton; Ambrose Heath's *Good Food*, illustrated by Edward Bawden; and, most exciting of all, *Len Deighton's Action Cookbook*.

I hope these recipes will bring pleasure to anyone who enjoys graphic art and simple, delicious, feel-good comfort food; I hope especially that they will be appreciated by those, like the many I have met, who find conventional recipes intimidating and difficult to use, but who can be instantly delighted by an intricate drawing, and will instinctively follow a sequence of images. There is a happy correlation, I have found, between the kind of honest cooking with everyday ingredients that I wanted this cookbook to contain, and the type of recipe uncomplicated enough to be illustrated on a single page in a certain number of frames. These recipes are designed, not to test the capabilities of the dedicated domestic chef, but rather to encourage everyone to try cooking for themselves, their families and their friends.

This book grew out of a sequence of twelve hand-drawn recipe cards (printed onto magnetic paper) that I sent, once a month throughout 2010, to friends and family in the UK and US. Here, that concept is expanded to fifty-two recipes, enough for you to try cooking something new each week for a whole year. Enjoy yourselves!

general principles

Ideally:

Butter used in cooking should be unsalted.
Caster sugar should be golden and unrefined.
Chocolate should have a high cocoa content: 70% for plain, 34% for milk.
Eggs should be large, free-range, and preferably organic.
Parmesan cheese should be freshly grated.
Pepper should be freshly, coarsely ground.
Salt should be the flaky, crumbly, from-the-sea kind (e.g. Maldon).

NB:
1tsp = 5ml
2tsp = 1 dessertspoon
3tsp = 1 tbsp
1tbsp = 15ml

Imperial to Metric
1 oz = 25g
4 oz = 110g
8 oz = 225g
12 oz = 350g
1lb = 450g

1 fl.oz = 30ml
2 fl.oz = 55ml
5 fl.oz or 1/4pt = 150ml
10 fl.oz or 1/2pt = 275ml
20 fl.oz or 1pt =600ml

American spoon measures
1 level tablespoon flour = 15g flour
1 heaped tablespoon flour = 28g flour
1 level tablespoon sugar = 28g sugar
1 level tablespoon butter = 15g butter

American solid measures
1 cup rice U.S. = 225g rice
1 cup flour U.S. = 115g flour
1 cup butter U.S. = 225g butter
1 stick butter U.S. = 115g butter
1 cup dried fruit U.S. = 225g dried fruit
1 cup brown sugar U.S. = 180g brown sugar
1 cup granulated sugar U.S. = 225g granulated sugar

American liquid measures
¼ cup U.S. = 50ml
½ cup U.S. = 120ml
¾ cup U.S. = 175ml
1 cup U.S. = 275ml
1 pint U.S. = 450ml
1 quart U.S. = 1litre

temperature conversion table

CELCIUS	FAHRENHEIT	GAS MARK
130	250	½
140	275	1
150	300	2
160	325	3
180	350	4
190	375	5
200	400	6
220	425	7
230	450	8
240	475	9
260	500	10

The oven temperatures given in the recipes apply to non fan-assisted ovens.
If you use a fan or convection oven, reduce the temperature by 15°C.

carrot & thyme soup
chicken noodle soup
lentil soup
mushroom soup
tomato soup
vichyssoise

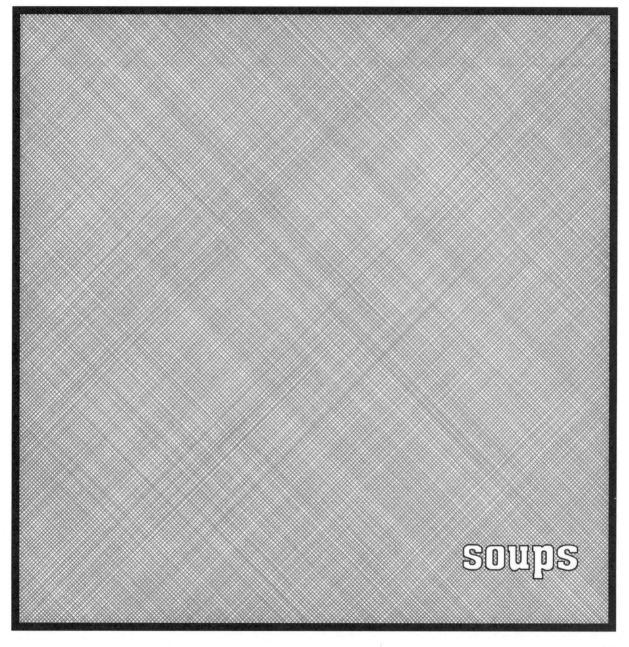

soups

carrot & thyme soup

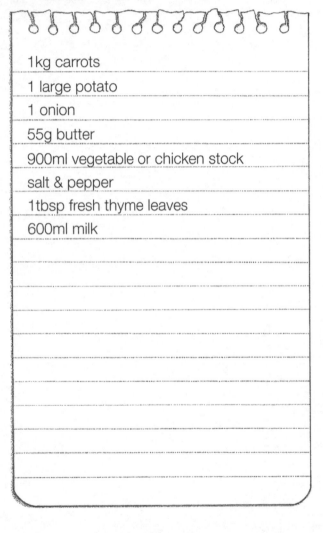

1kg carrots

1 large potato

1 onion

55g butter

900ml vegetable or chicken stock

salt & pepper

1tbsp fresh thyme leaves

600ml milk

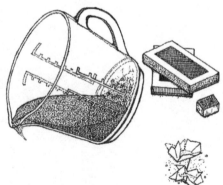

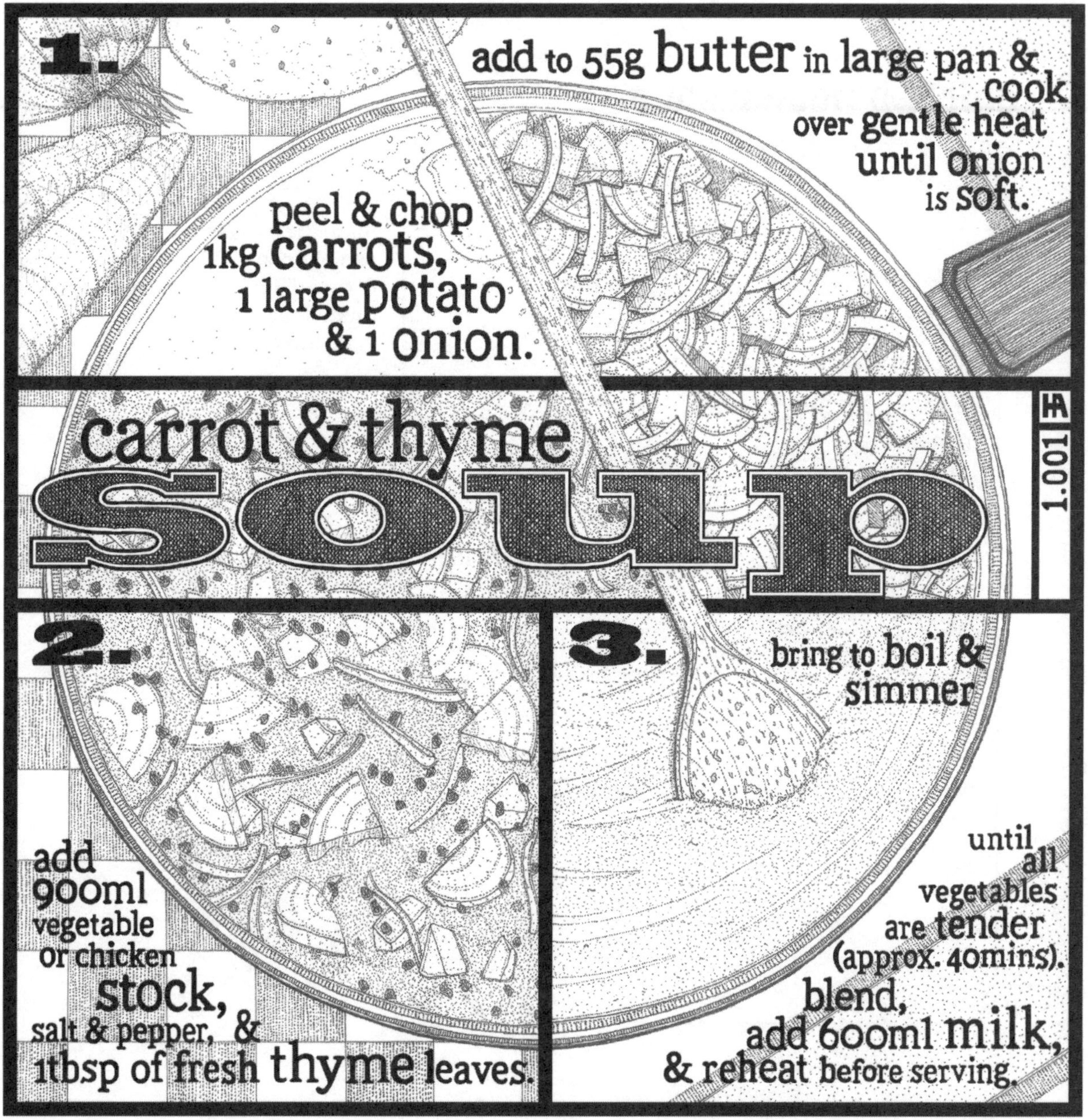
1.
add to 55g butter in large pan & cook over gentle heat until onion is soft.
peel & chop 1kg carrots, 1 large potato & 1 onion.
carrot & thyme
soup
1.001
2.
add 900ml vegetable or chicken stock, salt & pepper, & 1tbsp of fresh thyme leaves.
3.
bring to boil & simmer
until all vegetables are tender (approx. 40mins).
blend, add 600ml milk, & reheat before serving.

chicken noodle soup

serves 6

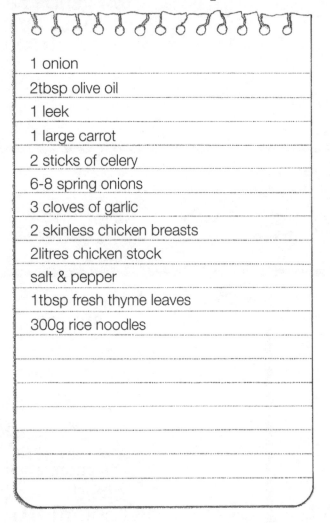

1 onion

2tbsp olive oil

1 leek

1 large carrot

2 sticks of celery

6-8 spring onions

3 cloves of garlic

2 skinless chicken breasts

2litres chicken stock

salt & pepper

1tbsp fresh thyme leaves

300g rice noodles

for a spicier version,
use 1 green chilli pepper
& 1 medium lump of ginger
(both finely chopped)
instead of thyme leaves.

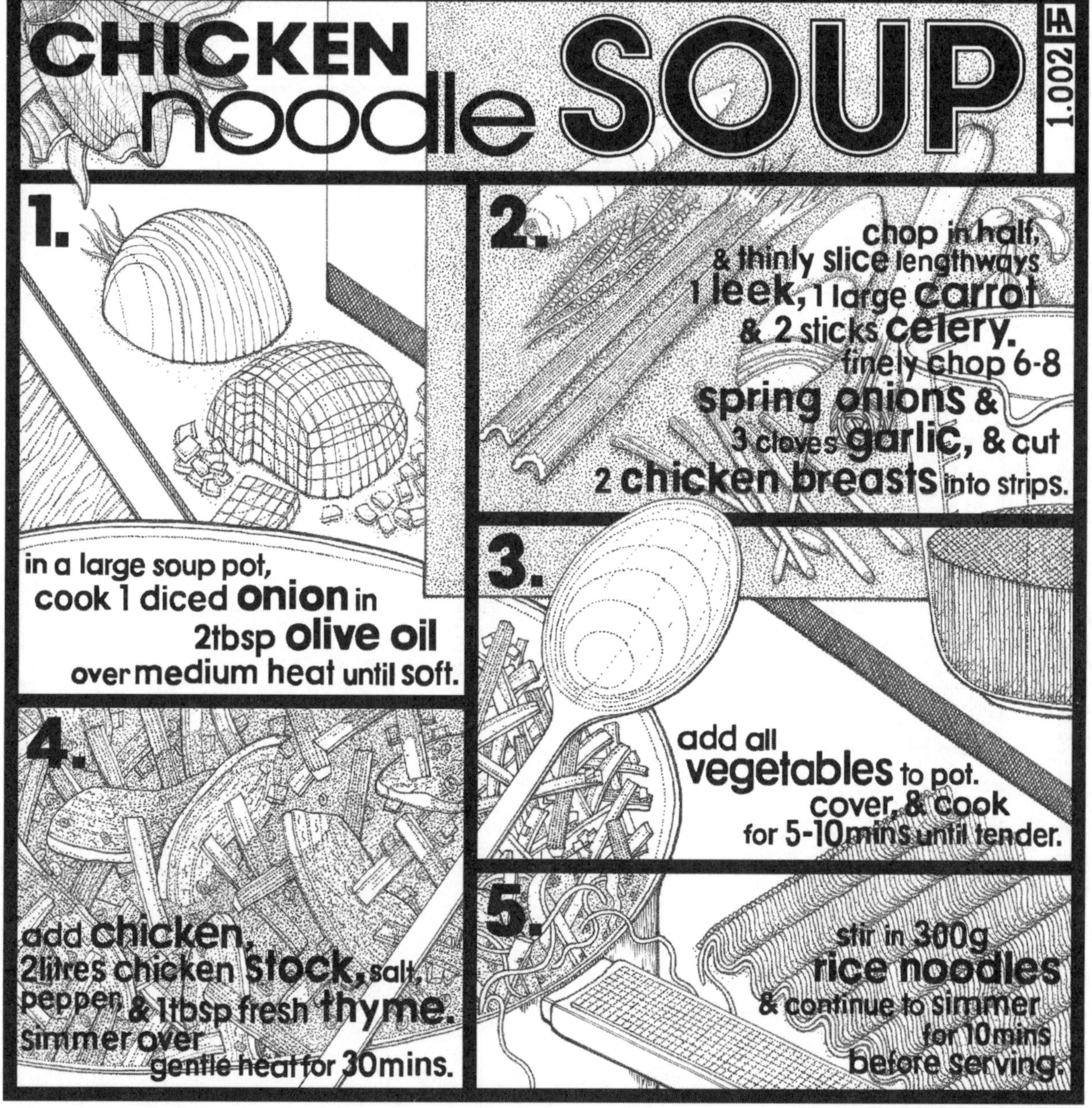
CHICKEN noodle SOUP
1.002
1.
in a large soup pot,
cook 1 diced onion in
2tbsp olive oil
over medium heat until soft.
2.
chop in half,
& thinly slice lengthways
1 leek, 1 large carrot
& 2 sticks celery.
finely chop 6-8
spring onions &
3 cloves garlic, & cut
2 chicken breasts into strips.
3.
add all
vegetables to pot.
cover, & cook
for 5-10mins until tender.
4.
add chicken,
2litres chicken stock, salt,
pepper, & 1tbsp fresh thyme.
simmer over
gentle heat for 30mins.
5.
stir in 300g
rice noodles
& continue to simmer
for 10mins
before serving.

lentil soup

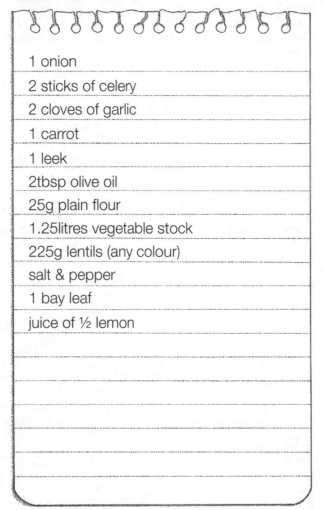

1 onion

2 sticks of celery

2 cloves of garlic

1 carrot

1 leek

2tbsp olive oil

25g plain flour

1.25litres vegetable stock

225g lentils (any colour)

salt & pepper

1 bay leaf

juice of ½ lemon

for a chunkier, heartier version use a parsnip instead of leek, and don't blend soup before serving.

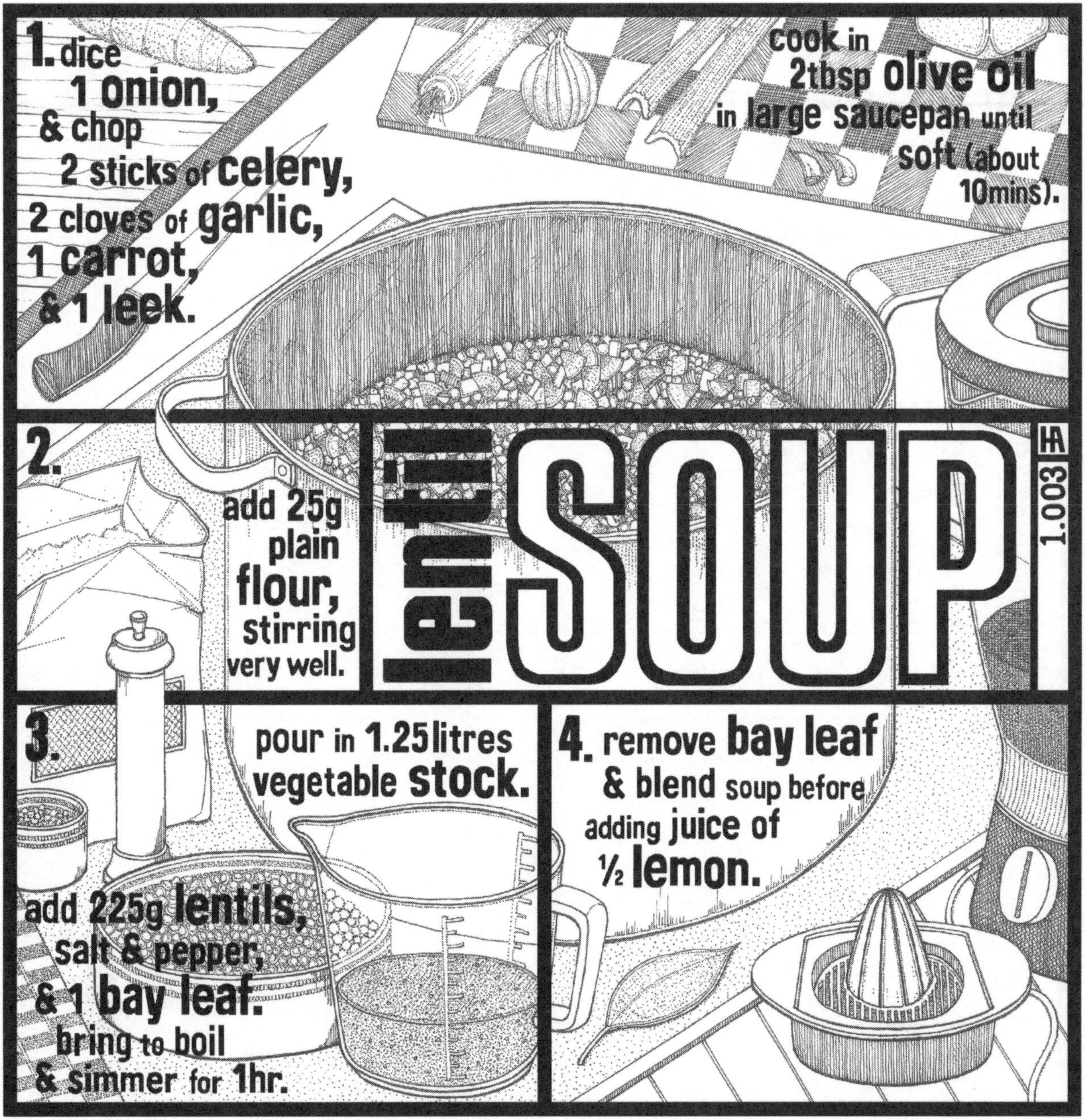
1. dice 1 onion, & chop 2 sticks of celery, 2 cloves of garlic, 1 carrot, & 1 leek.
cook in 2tbsp olive oil in large saucepan until soft (about 10mins).
2. add 25g plain flour, stirring very well.
lentil SOUP
1.003
3. pour in 1.25litres vegetable stock.
add 225g lentils, salt & pepper, & 1 bay leaf. bring to boil & simmer for 1hr.
4. remove bay leaf & blend soup before adding juice of ½ lemon.

mushroom soup

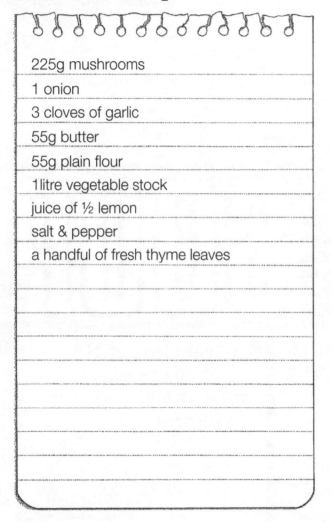

225g mushrooms

1 onion

3 cloves of garlic

55g butter

55g plain flour

1 litre vegetable stock

juice of ½ lemon

salt & pepper

a handful of fresh thyme leaves

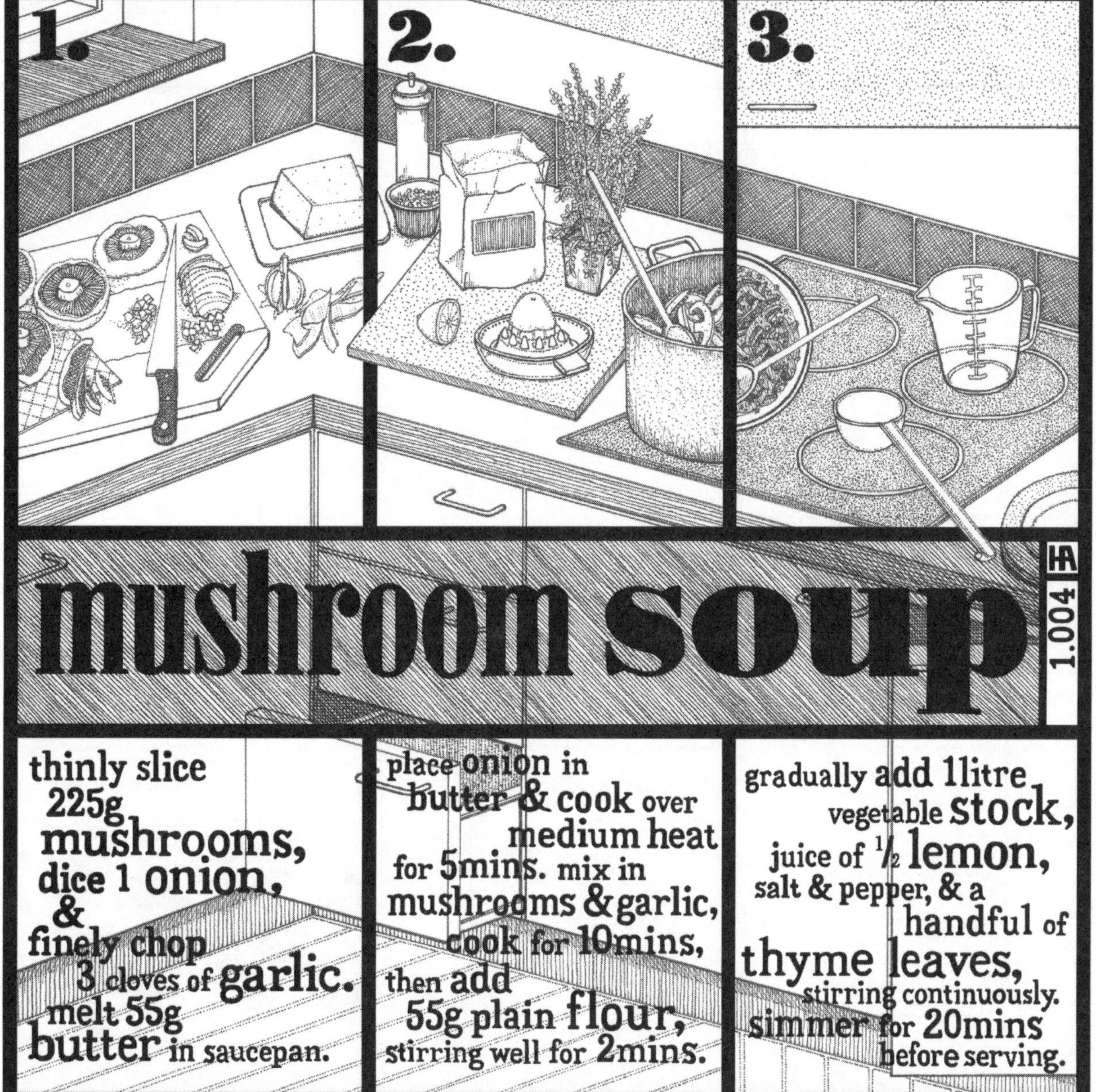
1.
2.
3.
mushroom soup
HA
1.004
thinly slice 225g mushrooms, dice 1 onion, & finely chop 3 cloves of garlic. melt 55g butter in saucepan.
place onion in butter & cook over medium heat for 5mins. mix in mushrooms & garlic, cook for 10mins, then add 55g plain flour, stirring well for 2mins.
gradually add 1litre vegetable stock, juice of ½ lemon, salt & pepper, & a handful of thyme leaves, stirring continuously. simmer for 20mins before serving.

tomato soup

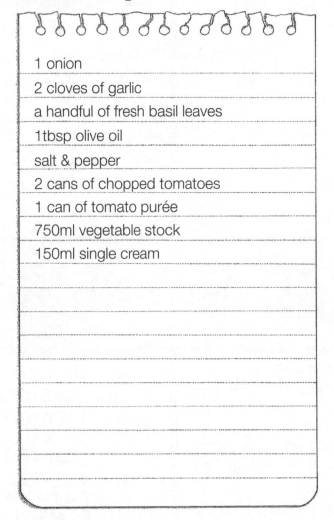

1 onion

2 cloves of garlic

a handful of fresh basil leaves

1tbsp olive oil

salt & pepper

2 cans of chopped tomatoes

1 can of tomato purée

750ml vegetable stock

150ml single cream

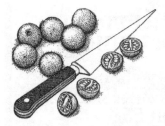

bolognese sauce
chilli con carne
jambalaya
kedgeree
pesto
risotto
spaghetti alla carbonara
tomato sauce

TOMATO SOUP

1. finely chop **1 onion,** 2 cloves of **garlic,** & a handful of fresh **basil leaves.**

2. fry onion over medium heat in 1tbsp **olive oil** in large pot until **soft.**

3. add garlic & seasoning, & continue to fry for **2-3mins** before adding **2 cans** of **chopped tomatoes** (incl. juice), **1 can** of **tomato purée,** & 750ml **vegetable stock.**

4. bring to **boil** & then simmer for **30mins.**

5. blend soup, then add **150ml** single **cream** & basil before serving.

vichysoisse

serves 4-6

500g leeks
2 large onions
500g potatoes
50g butter
1.25litres vegetable or chicken stock
salt & pepper
150ml single cream
1 bunch of fresh chives

can be served hot or cold.

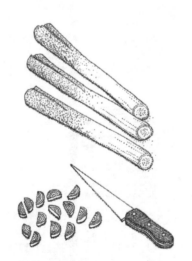

vichyssoise

1. finely chop 500g leeks & 2 large onions.

2. melt 50g butter in large pan, add leeks & onions, & fry gently (with lid on pan) for 10mins stirring occasionally.

3. add potatoes & cook for an additional 5mins.

4. peel & dice 500g potatoes. stir in 1-1/4litre vegetable or chicken stock. add salt & pepper.

5. simmer gently for 30-40 mins, blend. add 150ml single cream, additional seasoning if required, & finely chopped bunch of chives before serving.

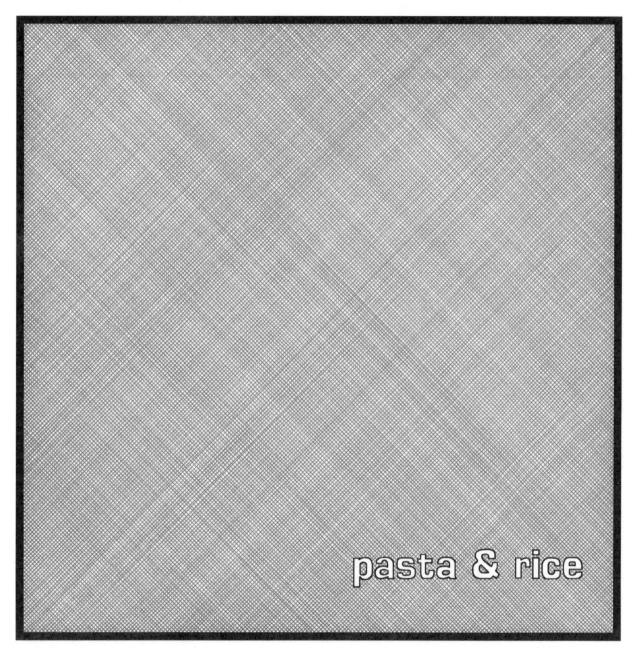

pasta & rice

bolognese sauce

serves 4

- 2 onions
- 3 cloves of garlic
- 250g mushrooms
- 3tbsp olive oil
- 500g lean beef mince
- 2 cans of tomatoes
- 1 can of tomato purée
- 1tsp sugar
- salt & pepper
- 1½tsp chilli flakes
- 2 bay leaves
- a handful of fresh rosemary
- 1 large sprig of fresh thyme
- 400g pasta (to serve)
- freshly grated parmesan (to serve)

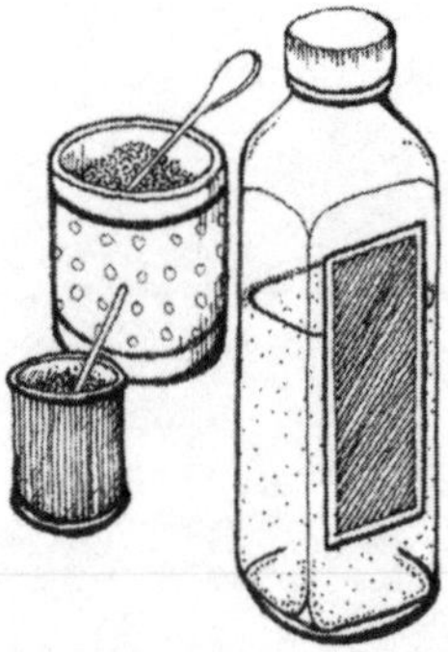

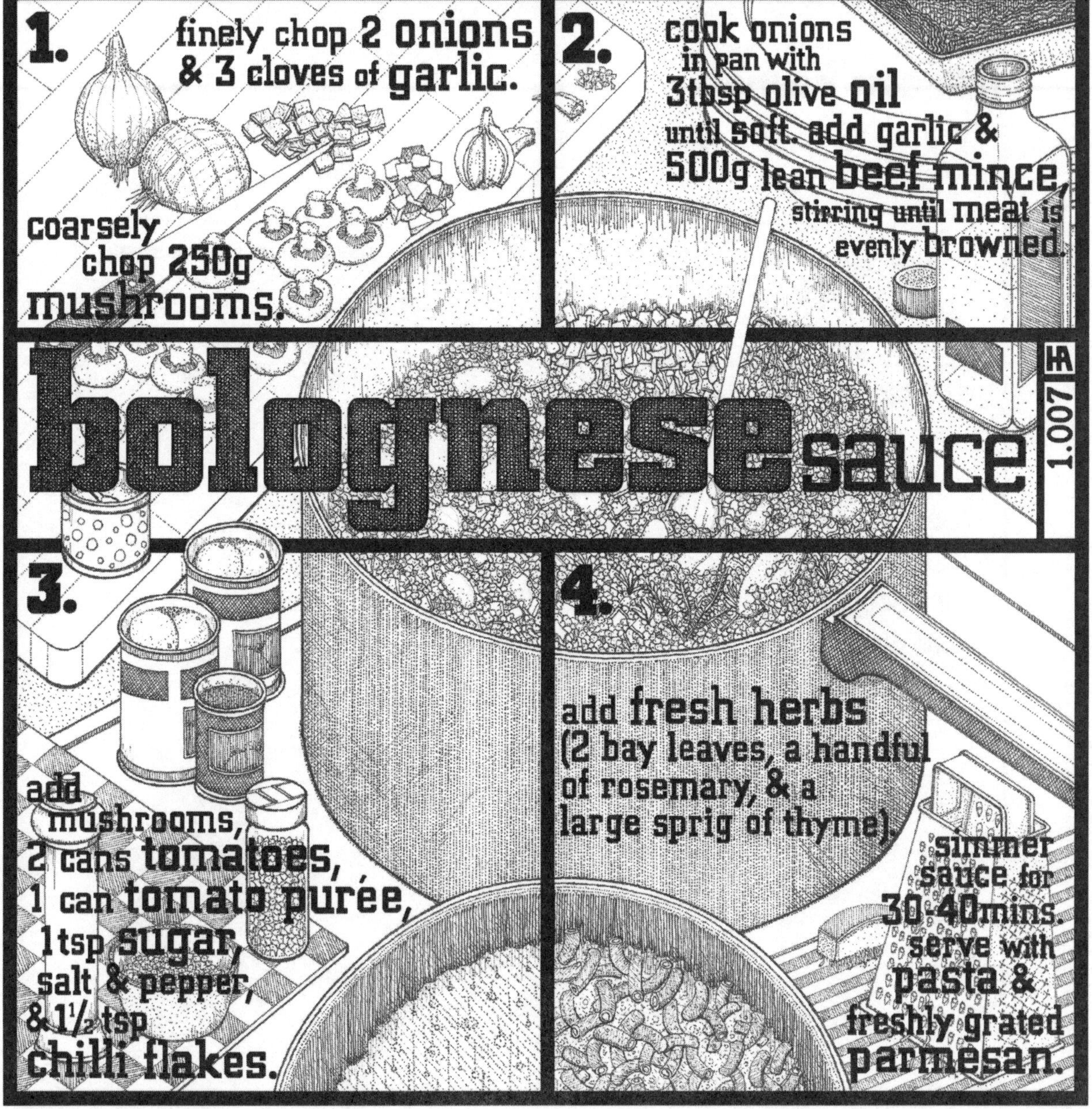
1.
finely chop 2 onions & 3 cloves of garlic.
coarsely chop 250g mushrooms.
2.
cook onions in pan with 3tbsp olive oil until soft. add garlic & 500g lean beef mince, stirring until meat is evenly browned.
bolognese sauce
HA
1.007
3.
add mushrooms, 2 cans tomatoes, 1 can tomato purée, 1tsp sugar, salt & pepper, & 1½ tsp chilli flakes.
4.
add fresh herbs (2 bay leaves, a handful of rosemary, & a large sprig of thyme).
simmer sauce for 30-40mins. serve with pasta & freshly grated parmesan.

chilli con carne

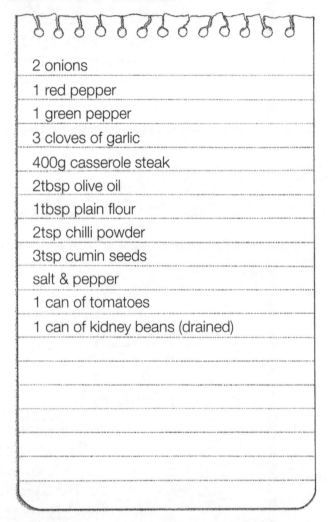

2 onions

1 red pepper

1 green pepper

3 cloves of garlic

400g casserole steak

2tbsp olive oil

1tbsp plain flour

2tsp chilli powder

3tsp cumin seeds

salt & pepper

1 can of tomatoes

1 can of kidney beans (drained)

can use lean beef mince instead of casserole steak.

can substitute 1 red chilli pepper (deseeded to taste) for the chilli powder.

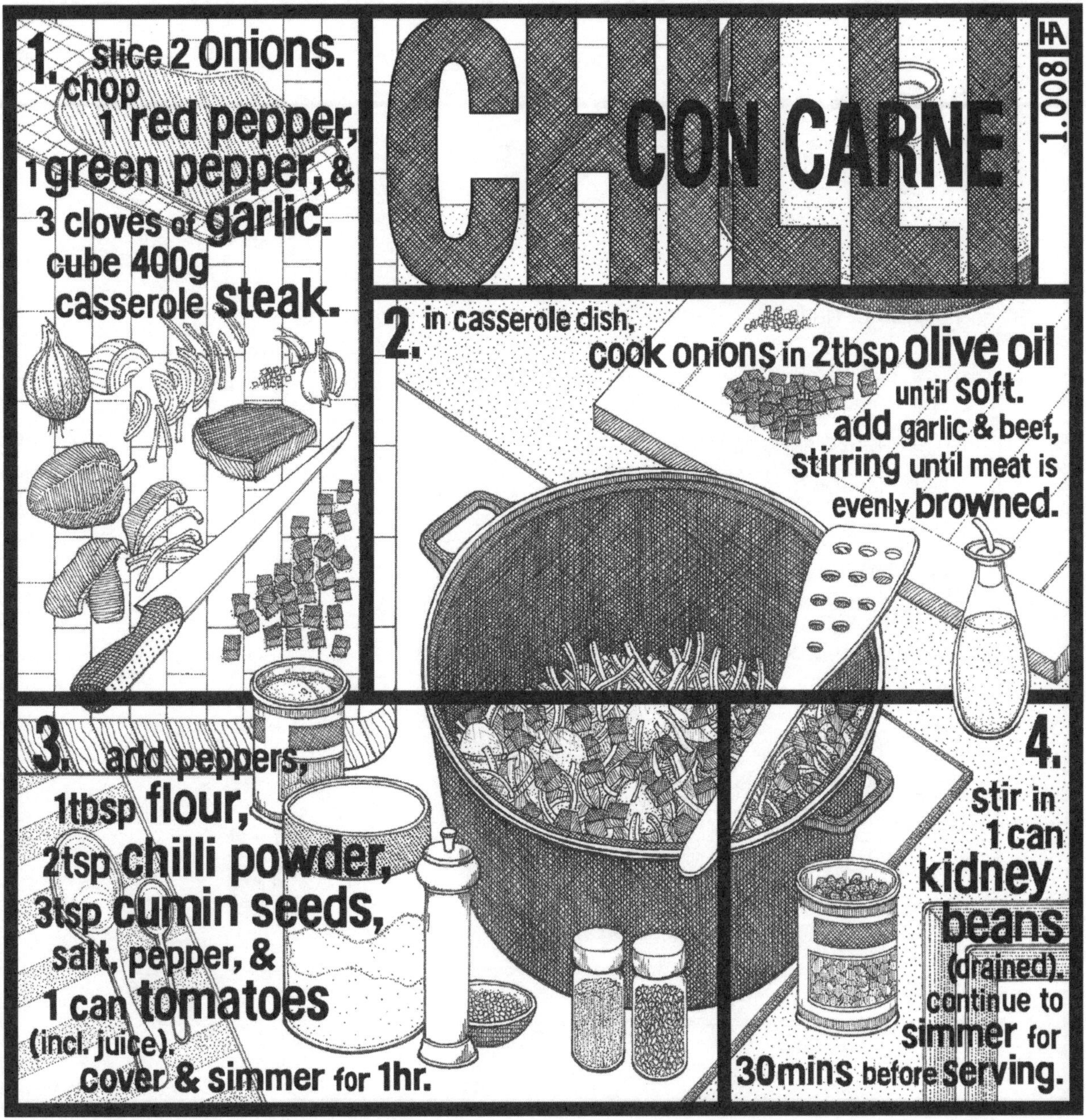
CHILLI CON CARNE
1.008
1. slice 2 onions.
chop 1 red pepper,
1 green pepper, &
3 cloves of garlic.
cube 400g casserole steak.
2. in casserole dish,
cook onions in 2tbsp olive oil until soft.
add garlic & beef,
stirring until meat is evenly browned.
3. add peppers,
1tbsp flour,
2tsp chilli powder,
3tsp cumin seeds,
salt, pepper, &
1 can tomatoes
(incl. juice).
cover & simmer for 1hr.
4. stir in
1 can
kidney beans
(drained).
continue to simmer for
30mins before serving.

jambalaya

serves 4

- 1 onion
- 2 peppers
- 3 cloves of garlic
- 1 red chilli pepper
- 2 skinless chicken breasts
- 125g chorizo sausage
- 1tbsp olive oil
- salt & pepper
- 1tsp cayenne pepper
- 1tsp paprika
- 1 can of tomatoes
- 568ml water
- 175g peeled raw king prawns
- 250g long grain white rice
- 1 lemon (to serve)
- a handful of fresh parsley (to serve)

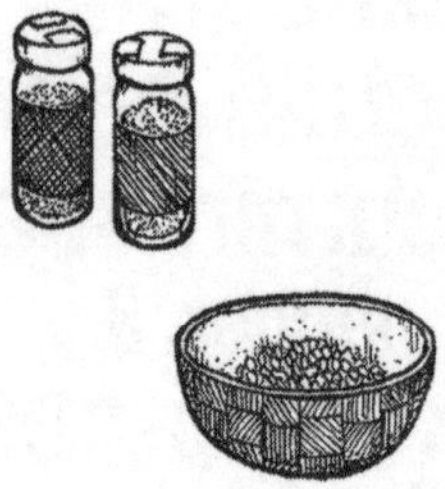

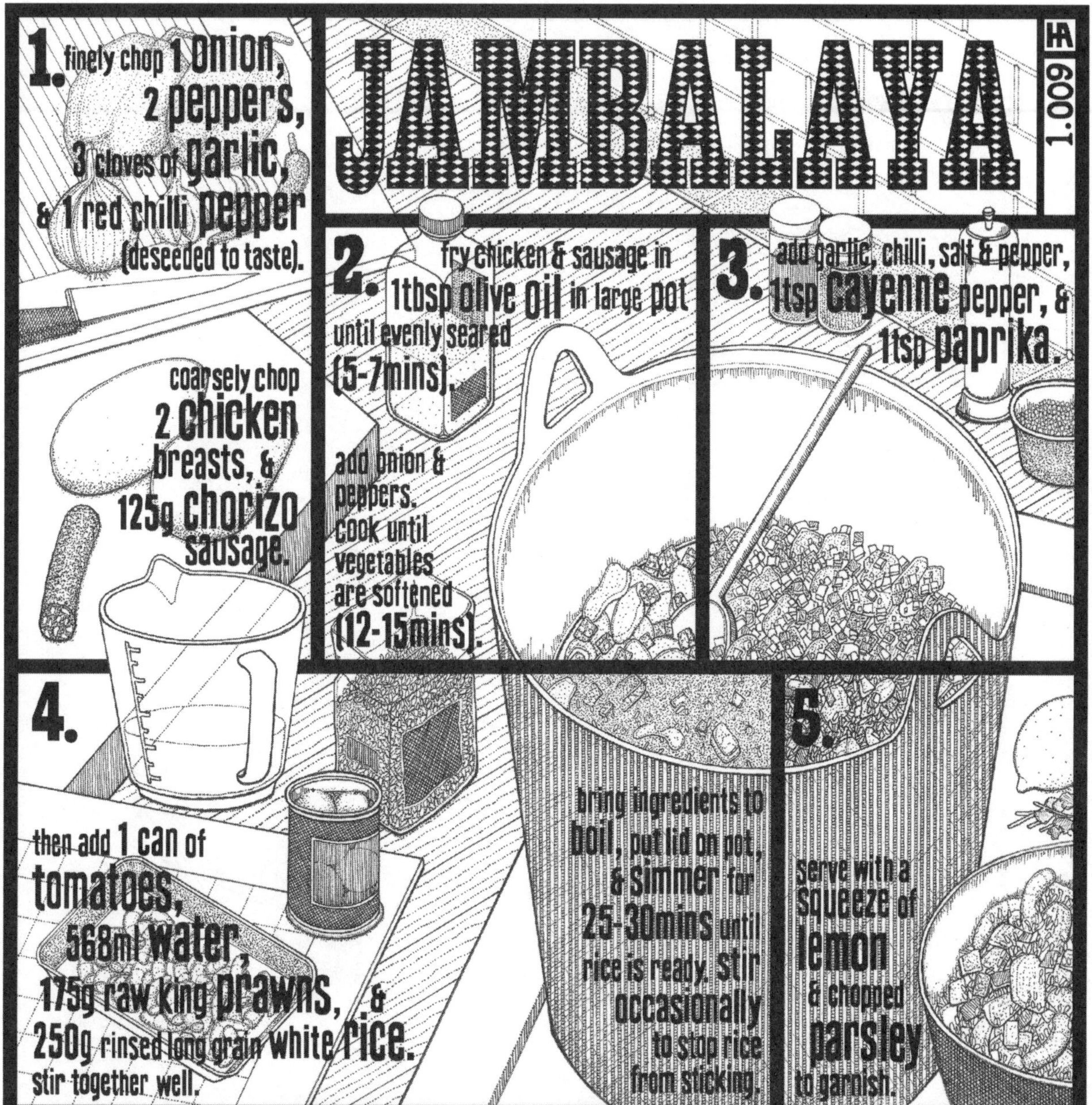
JAMBALAYA
HA
1.009
1. finely chop 1 onion, 2 peppers, 3 cloves of garlic, & 1 red chilli pepper (deseeded to taste).
coarsely chop 2 chicken breasts, & 125g chorizo sausage.
2. fry chicken & sausage in 1tbsp olive oil in large pot until evenly seared (5-7mins).
add onion & peppers. cook until vegetables are softened (12-15mins).
3. add garlic, chilli, salt & pepper, 1tsp cayenne pepper, & 1tsp paprika.
4.
then add 1 can of tomatoes, 568ml water, 175g raw king prawns, & 250g rinsed long grain white rice. stir together well.
bring ingredients to boil, put lid on pot, & simmer for 25-30mins until rice is ready. stir occasionally to stop rice from sticking.
5.
serve with a squeeze of lemon & chopped parsley to garnish.

kedgeree

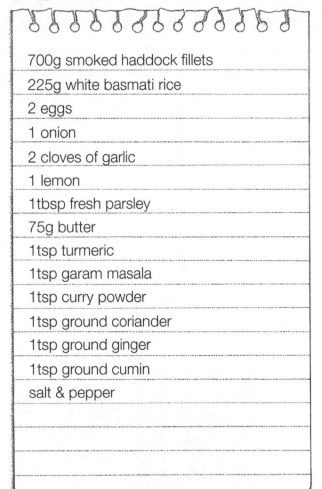

700g smoked haddock fillets

225g white basmati rice

2 eggs

1 onion

2 cloves of garlic

1 lemon

1tbsp fresh parsley

75g butter

1tsp turmeric

1tsp garam masala

1tsp curry powder

1tsp ground coriander

1tsp ground ginger

1tsp ground cumin

salt & pepper

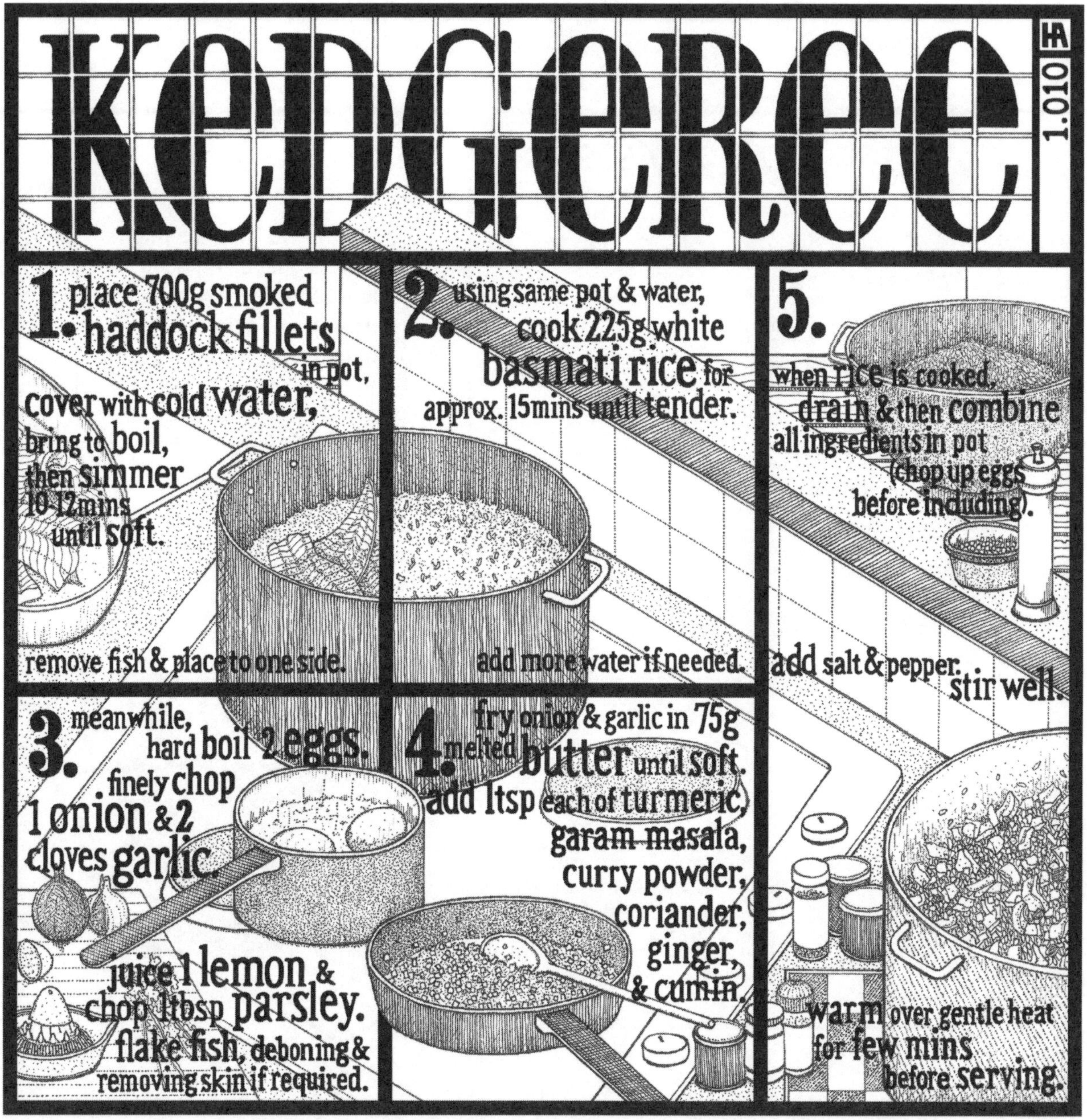
KEDGEREE
HA
1.010
1. place 700g smoked haddock fillets in pot,
cover with cold water,
bring to boil,
then simmer 10-12mins until soft.
remove fish & place to one side.
2. using same pot & water,
cook 225g white basmati rice for approx. 15mins until tender.
add more water if needed.
3. meanwhile, hard boil 2 eggs.
finely chop 1 onion & 2 cloves garlic.
juice 1 lemon & chop 1tbsp parsley.
flake fish, deboning & removing skin if required.
4. fry onion & garlic in 75g melted butter until soft.
add 1tsp each of turmeric,
garam masala,
curry powder,
coriander,
ginger,
& cumin.
5. when rice is cooked, drain & then combine all ingredients in pot
(chop up eggs before including).
add salt & pepper. stir well.
warm over gentle heat for few mins before serving.

pesto

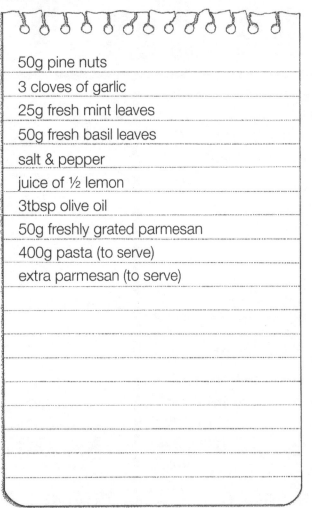

- 50g pine nuts
- 3 cloves of garlic
- 25g fresh mint leaves
- 50g fresh basil leaves
- salt & pepper
- juice of ½ lemon
- 3tbsp olive oil
- 50g freshly grated parmesan
- 400g pasta (to serve)
- extra parmesan (to serve)

alternative versions might include just using basil leaves (for a more typical pesto) or a different type of leaf, e.g. rocket.

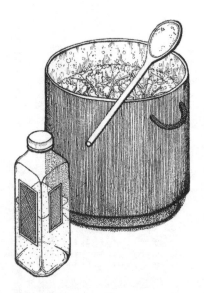

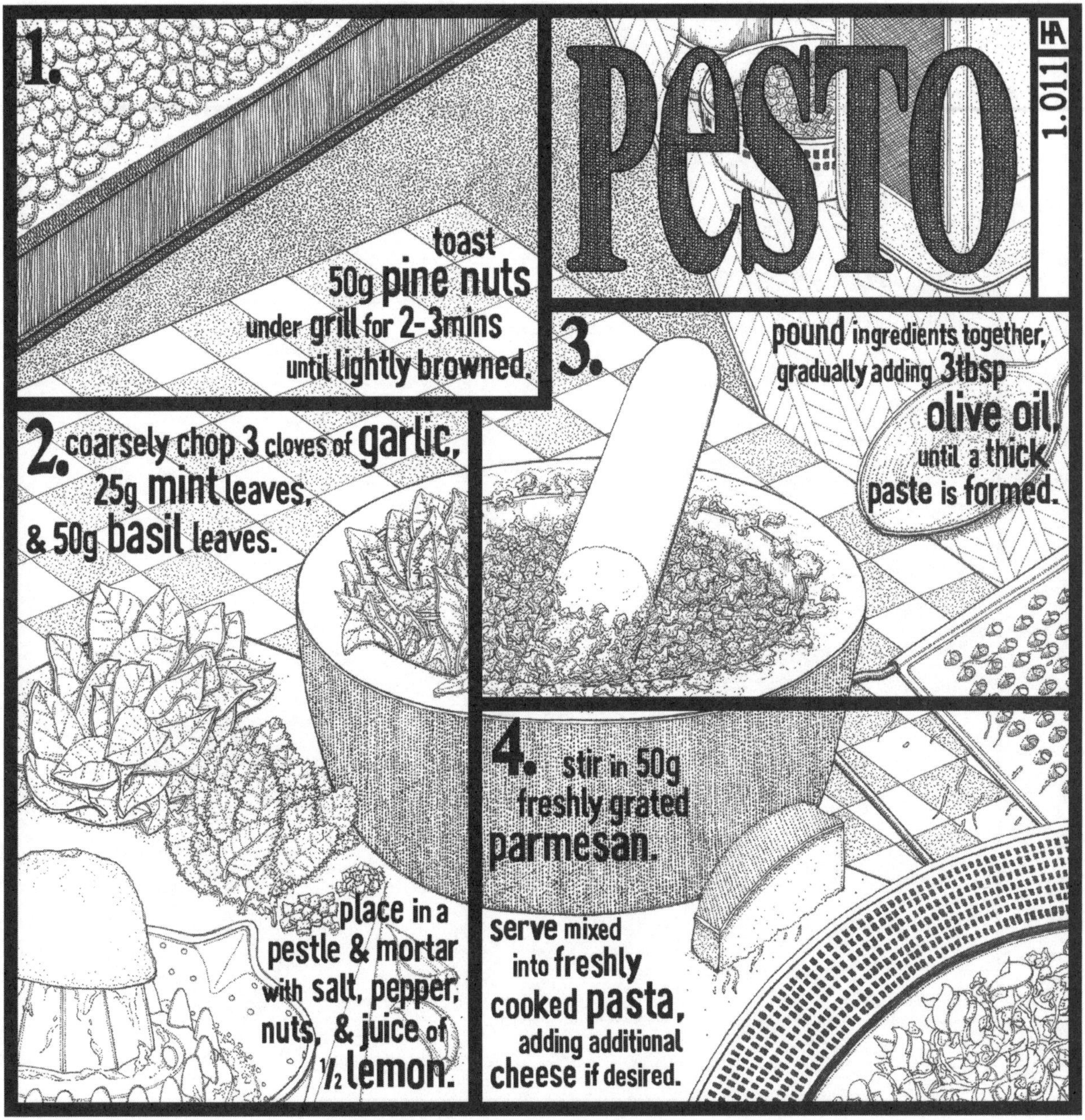
PESTO
HA 1.011
1.
toast
50g pine nuts
under grill for 2-3mins
until lightly browned.
2. coarsely chop 3 cloves of garlic,
25g mint leaves,
& 50g basil leaves.
place in a
pestle & mortar
with salt, pepper,
nuts, & juice of
½ lemon.
3.
pound ingredients together,
gradually adding 3tbsp
olive oil,
until a thick
paste is formed.
4. stir in 50g
freshly grated
parmesan.
serve mixed
into freshly
cooked pasta,
adding additional
cheese if desired.

risotto

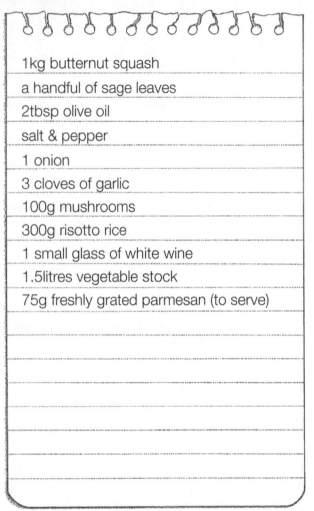

1kg butternut squash

a handful of sage leaves

2tbsp olive oil

salt & pepper

1 onion

3 cloves of garlic

100g mushrooms

300g risotto rice

1 small glass of white wine

1.5litres vegetable stock

75g freshly grated parmesan (to serve)

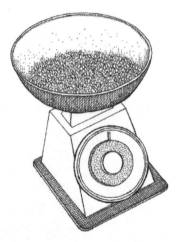

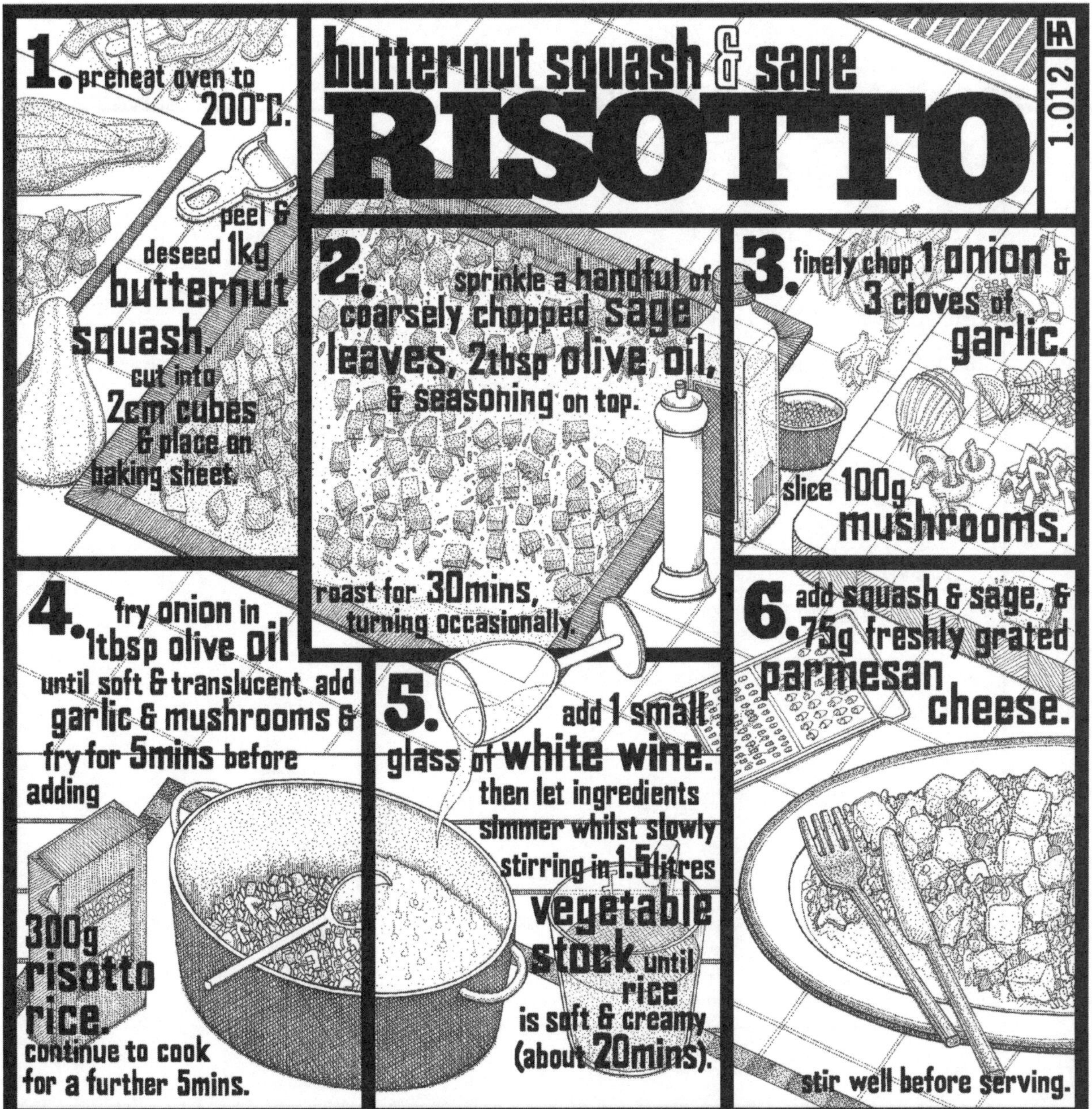
butternut squash & sage
RISOTTO
HA
1.012
1. preheat oven to 200°C.
peel & deseed 1kg butternut squash. cut into 2cm cubes & place on baking sheet.
2. sprinkle a handful of coarsely chopped sage leaves, 2tbsp olive oil, & seasoning on top.
roast for 30mins, turning occasionally.
3. finely chop 1 onion & 3 cloves of garlic.
slice 100g mushrooms.
4. fry onion in 1tbsp olive oil until soft & translucent. add garlic & mushrooms & fry for 5mins before adding
300g risotto rice.
continue to cook for a further 5mins.
5. add 1 small glass of white wine.
then let ingredients simmer whilst slowly stirring in 1.5litres vegetable stock until rice is soft & creamy (about 20mins).
6. add squash & sage, & 75g freshly grated parmesan cheese.
stir well before serving.

spaghetti alla carbonara

serves 2

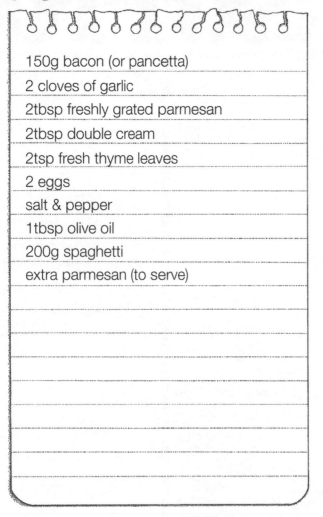

150g bacon (or pancetta)

2 cloves of garlic

2tbsp freshly grated parmesan

2tbsp double cream

2tsp fresh thyme leaves

2 eggs

salt & pepper

1tbsp olive oil

200g spaghetti

extra parmesan (to serve)

* add a splash of oil to the water to prevent the pasta from sticking together.

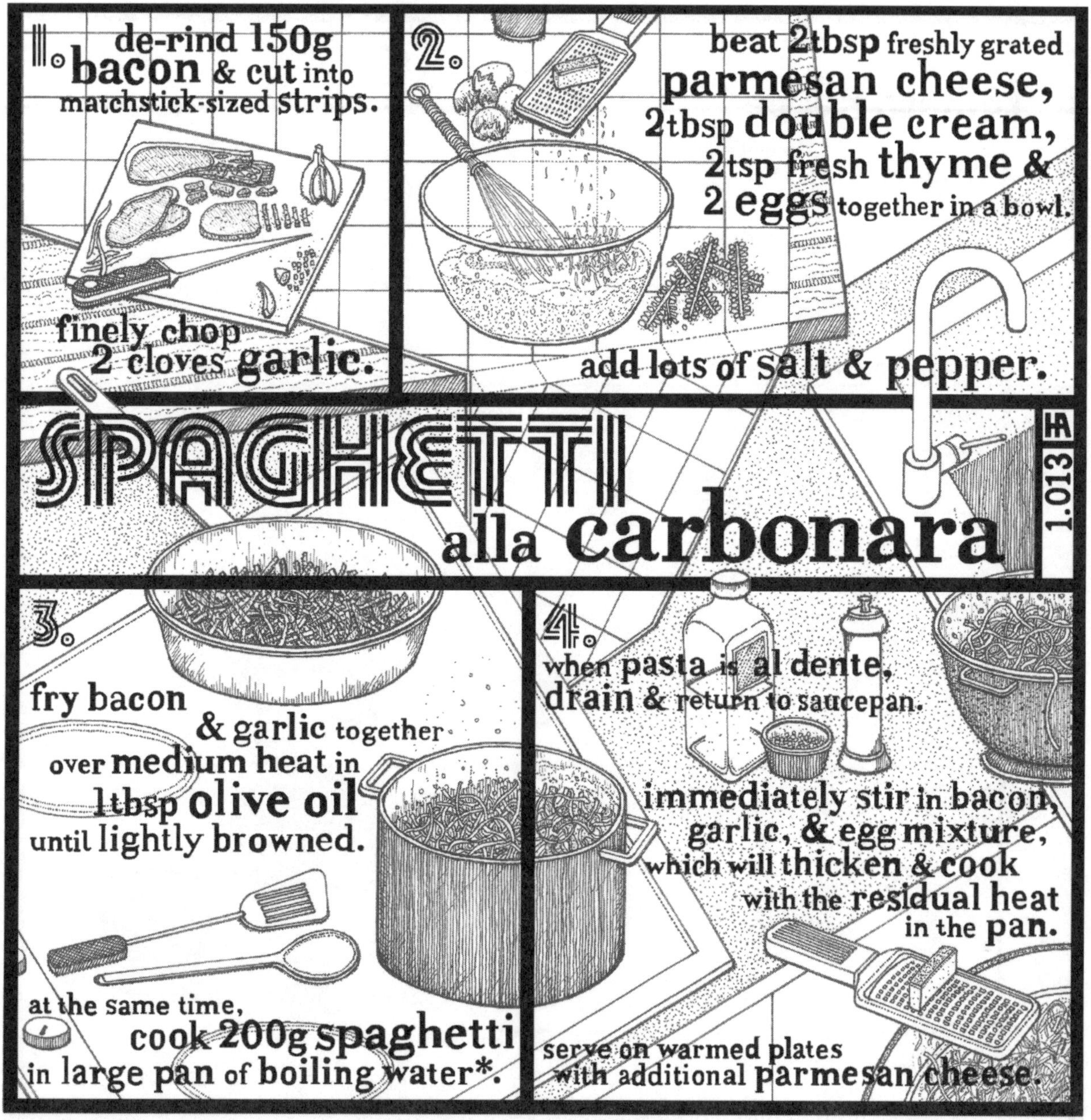
SPAGHETTI
alla carbonara
1.013
1. de-rind 150g bacon & cut into matchstick-sized strips.
finely chop 2 cloves garlic.
2. beat 2tbsp freshly grated parmesan cheese, 2tbsp double cream, 2tsp fresh thyme & 2 eggs together in a bowl.
add lots of salt & pepper.
3. fry bacon & garlic together over medium heat in 1tbsp olive oil until lightly browned.
at the same time, cook 200g spaghetti in large pan of boiling water*.
4. when pasta is al dente, drain & return to saucepan.
immediately stir in bacon, garlic, & egg mixture, which will thicken & cook with the residual heat in the pan.
serve on warmed plates with additional parmesan cheese.

tomato sauce

serves 4

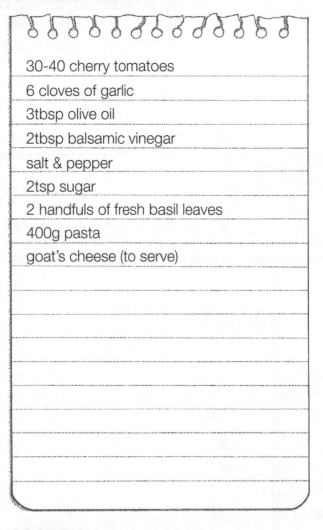

- 30-40 cherry tomatoes
- 6 cloves of garlic
- 3tbsp olive oil
- 2tbsp balsamic vinegar
- salt & pepper
- 2tsp sugar
- 2 handfuls of fresh basil leaves
- 400g pasta
- goat's cheese (to serve)

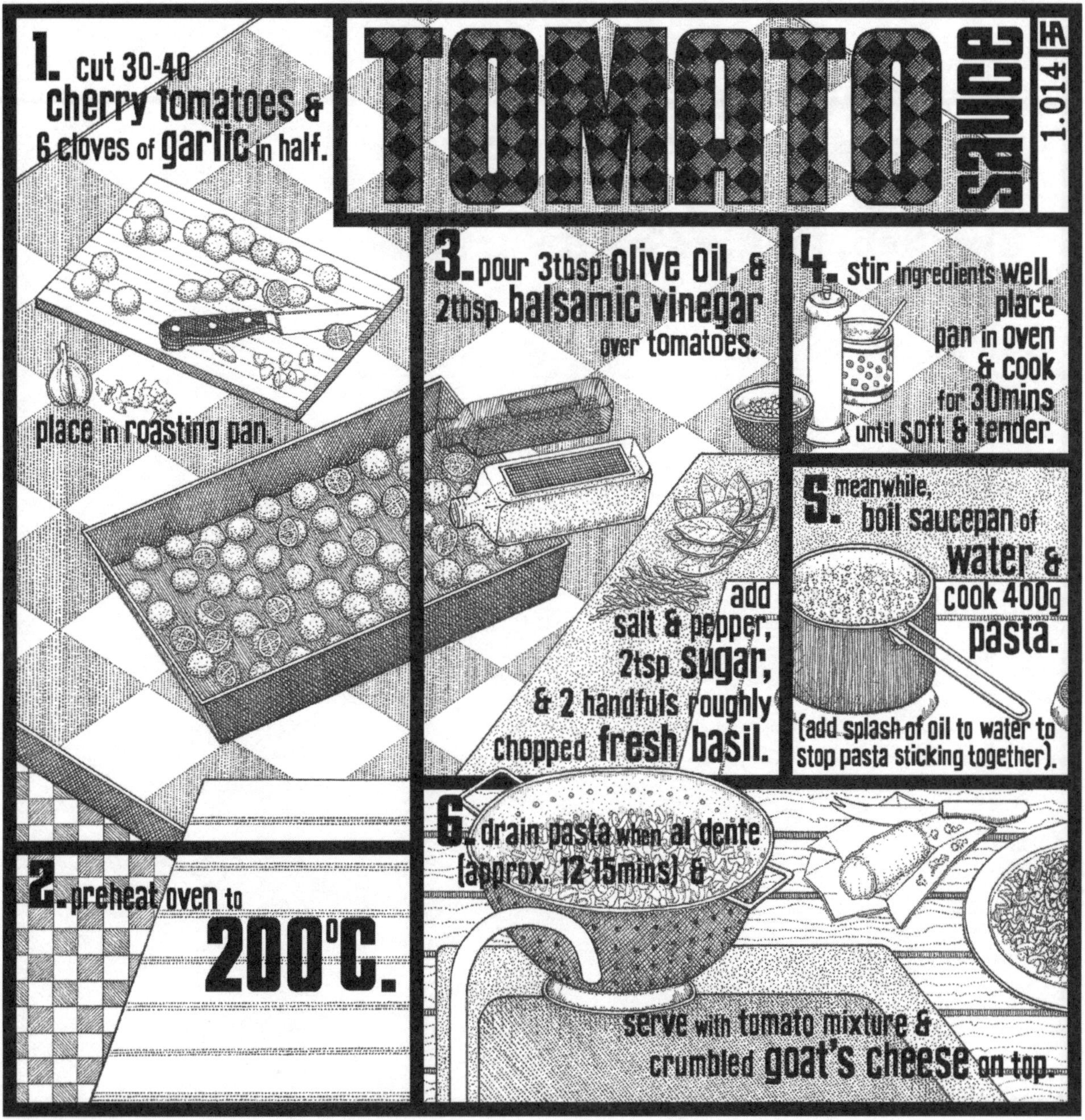
TOMATO sauce
1.014
1. cut 30-40 cherry tomatoes & 6 cloves of garlic in half.
place in roasting pan.
2. preheat oven to 200°C.
3. pour 3tbsp olive oil, & 2tbsp balsamic vinegar over tomatoes.
add salt & pepper, 2tsp sugar, & 2 handfuls roughly chopped fresh basil.
4. stir ingredients well. place pan in oven & cook for 30mins until soft & tender.
5. meanwhile, boil saucepan of water & cook 400g pasta.
(add splash of oil to water to stop pasta sticking together).
6. drain pasta when al dente (approx. 12-15mins) &
serve with tomato mixture & crumbled goat's cheese on top.

carbonnade du boeuf
cheese & bacon baked potatoes
chicken & mushroom pie
chicken, leek, & bacon crumble
sausage & bean casserole
shepherds' pie

main courses - meat

carbonnade du boeuf

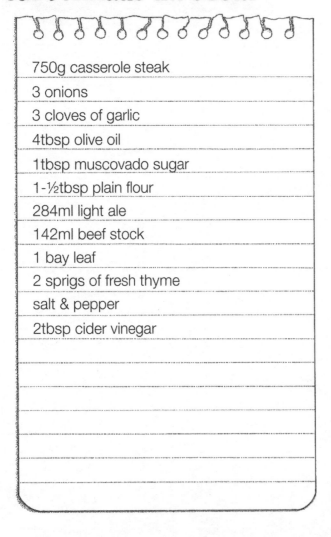

- 750g casserole steak
- 3 onions
- 3 cloves of garlic
- 4tbsp olive oil
- 1tbsp muscovado sugar
- 1-½tbsp plain flour
- 284ml light ale
- 142ml beef stock
- 1 bay leaf
- 2 sprigs of fresh thyme
- salt & pepper
- 2tbsp cider vinegar

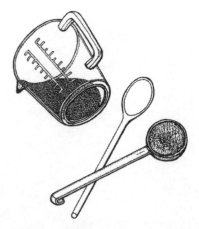

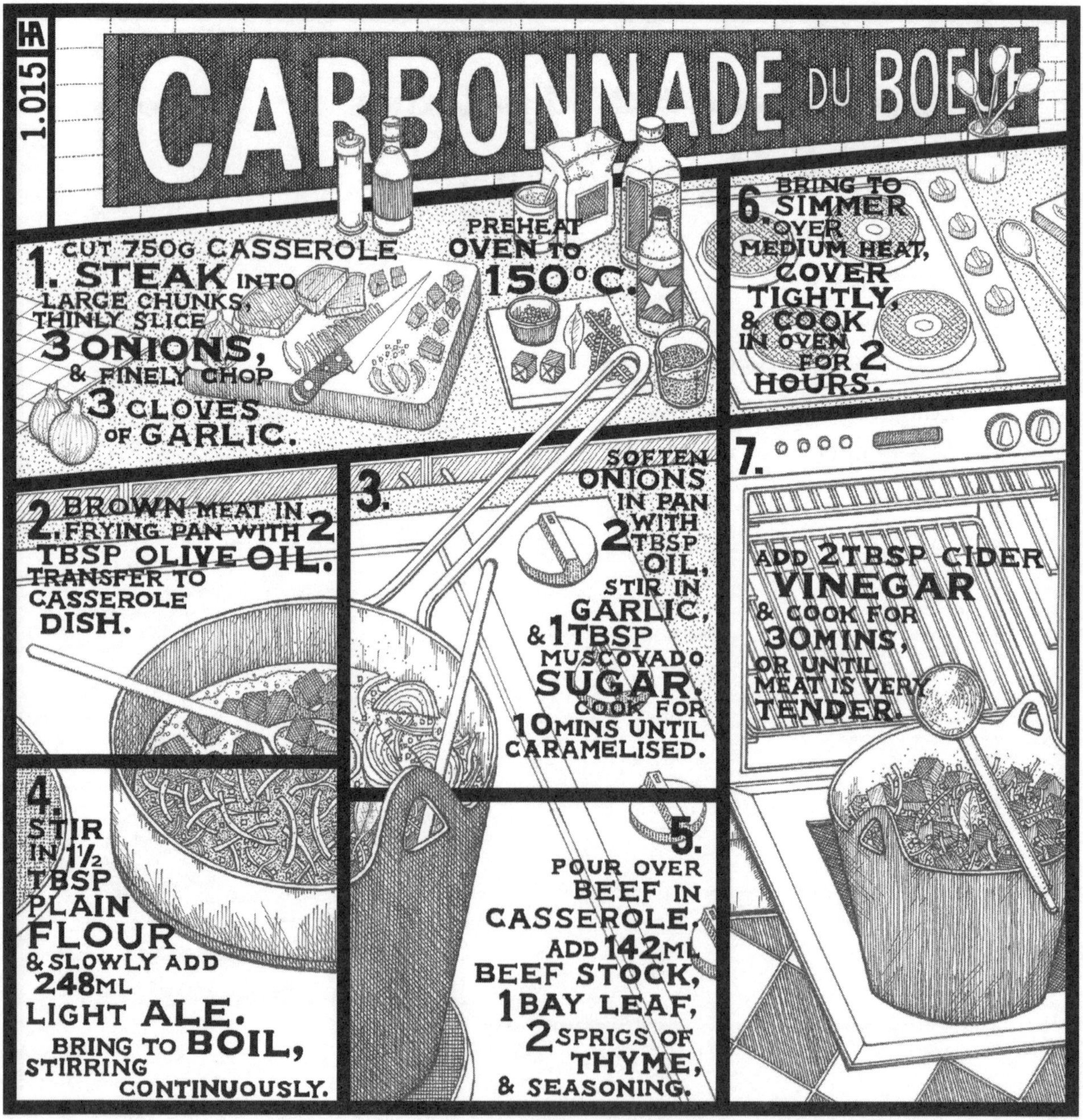

1.015
CARBONNADE DU BOEUF
1. CUT 750G CASSEROLE STEAK INTO LARGE CHUNKS, THINLY SLICE 3 ONIONS, & FINELY CHOP 3 CLOVES OF GARLIC.
PREHEAT OVEN TO 150°C.
2. BROWN MEAT IN FRYING PAN WITH 2 TBSP OLIVE OIL. TRANSFER TO CASSEROLE DISH.
3. SOFTEN ONIONS IN PAN WITH 2 TBSP OIL, STIR IN GARLIC, & 1 TBSP MUSCOVADO SUGAR. COOK FOR 10 MINS UNTIL CARAMELISED.
4. STIR IN 1½ TBSP PLAIN FLOUR & SLOWLY ADD 248ML LIGHT ALE. BRING TO BOIL, STIRRING CONTINUOUSLY.
5. POUR OVER BEEF IN CASSEROLE. ADD 142ML BEEF STOCK, 1 BAY LEAF, 2 SPRIGS OF THYME, & SEASONING.
6. BRING TO SIMMER OVER MEDIUM HEAT, COVER TIGHTLY, & COOK IN OVEN FOR 2 HOURS.
7. ADD 2 TBSP CIDER VINEGAR & COOK FOR 30 MINS, OR UNTIL MEAT IS VERY TENDER.

cheese & bacon baked potatoes

serves 1

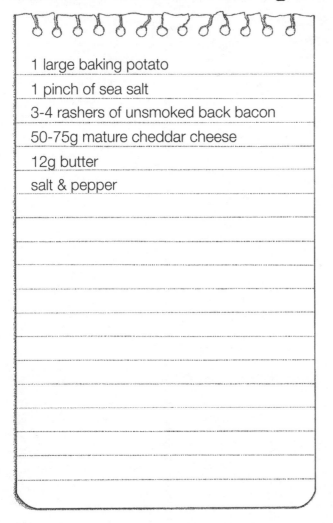

1 large baking potato

1 pinch of sea salt

3-4 rashers of unsmoked back bacon

50-75g mature cheddar cheese

12g butter

salt & pepper

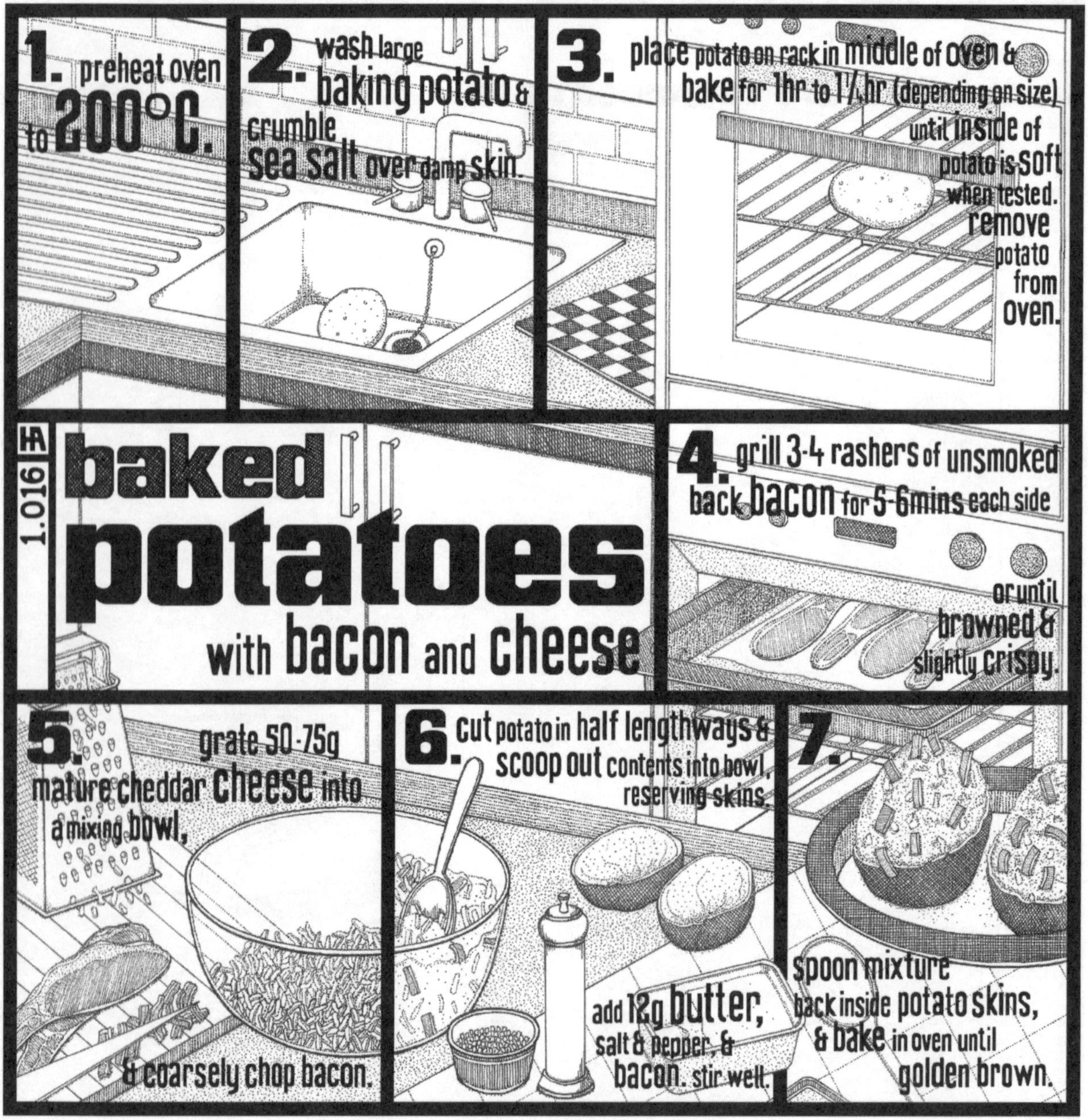
1.016
baked potatoes
with bacon and cheese
1. preheat oven to 200°C.
2. wash large baking potato & crumble sea salt over damp skin.
3. place potato on rack in middle of oven & bake for 1hr to 1¼hr (depending on size) until inside of potato is soft when tested. remove potato from oven.
4. grill 3-4 rashers of unsmoked back bacon for 5-6mins each side or until browned & slightly crispy.
5. grate 50-75g mature cheddar cheese into a mixing bowl, & coarsely chop bacon.
6. cut potato in half lengthways & scoop out contents into bowl, reserving skins.
add 12g butter, salt & pepper, & bacon. stir well.
7. spoon mixture back inside potato skins, & bake in oven until golden brown.

chicken & mushroom pie

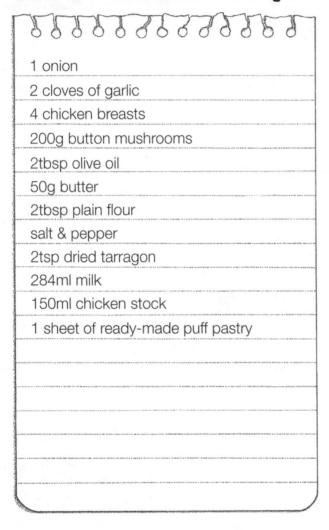

- 1 onion
- 2 cloves of garlic
- 4 chicken breasts
- 200g button mushrooms
- 2tbsp olive oil
- 50g butter
- 2tbsp plain flour
- salt & pepper
- 2tsp dried tarragon
- 284ml milk
- 150ml chicken stock
- 1 sheet of ready-made puff pastry

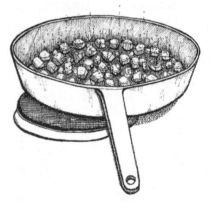

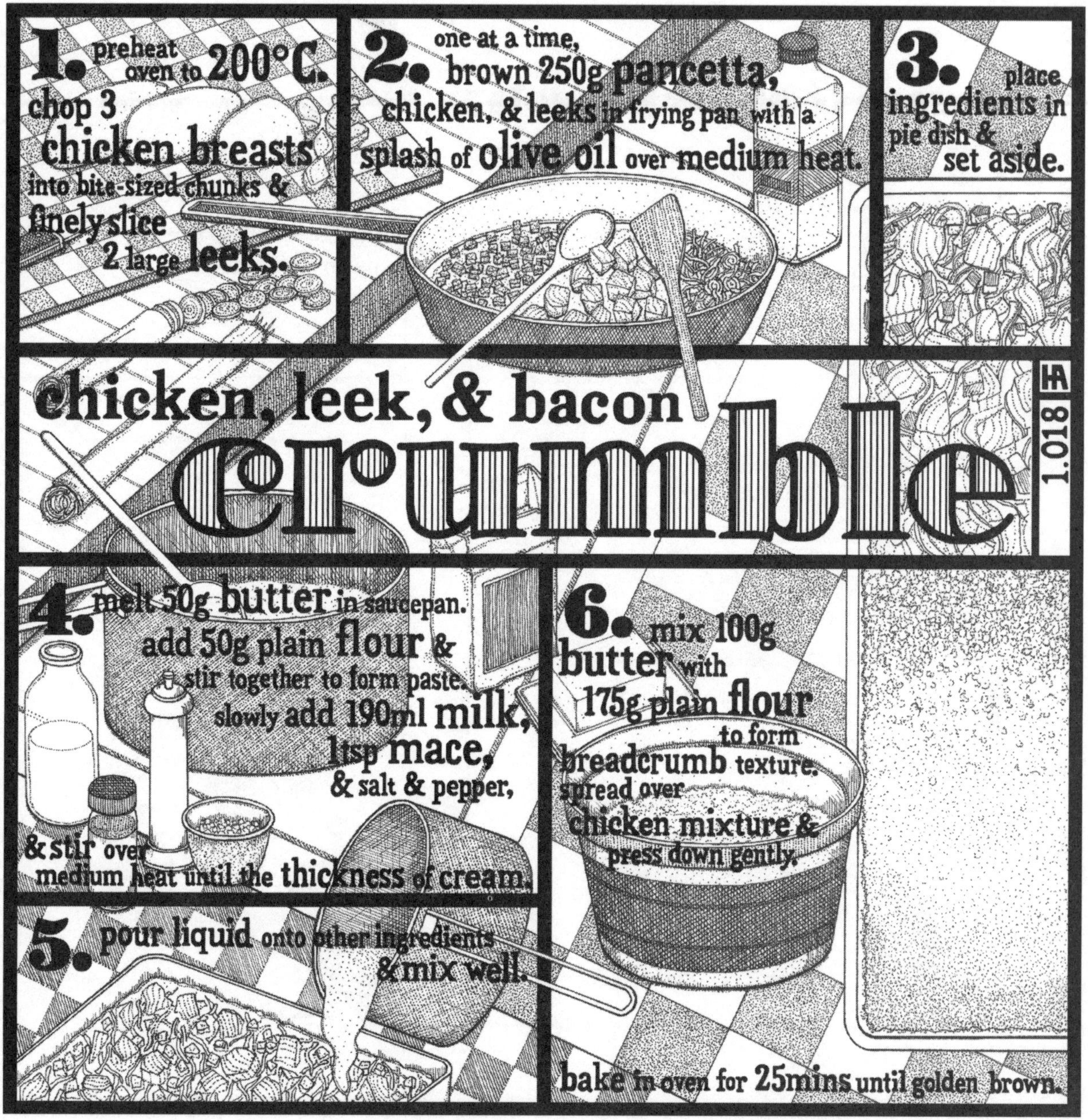
1. preheat oven to 200°C.
chop 3 chicken breasts into bite-sized chunks & finely slice 2 large leeks.
2. one at a time, brown 250g pancetta, chicken, & leeks in frying pan with a splash of olive oil over medium heat.
3. place ingredients in pie dish & set aside.
chicken, leek, & bacon
crumble
HA
1.018
4. melt 50g butter in saucepan. add 50g plain flour & stir together to form paste. slowly add 190ml milk, 1tsp mace, & salt & pepper, & stir over medium heat until the thickness of cream.
5. pour liquid onto other ingredients & mix well.
6. mix 100g butter with 175g plain flour to form breadcrumb texture. spread over chicken mixture & press down gently.
bake in oven for 25mins until golden brown.

sausage & bean casserole

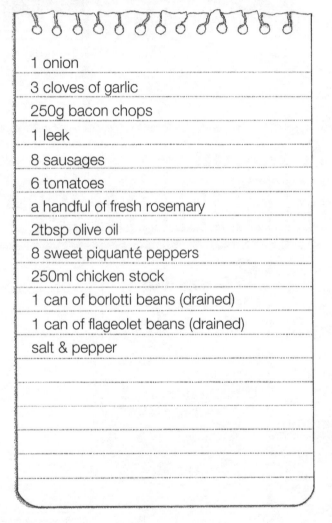

1 onion

3 cloves of garlic

250g bacon chops

1 leek

8 sausages

6 tomatoes

a handful of fresh rosemary

2tbsp olive oil

8 sweet piquanté peppers

250ml chicken stock

1 can of borlotti beans (drained)

1 can of flageolet beans (drained)

salt & pepper

pancetta can be used as an alternative to the bacon chops.

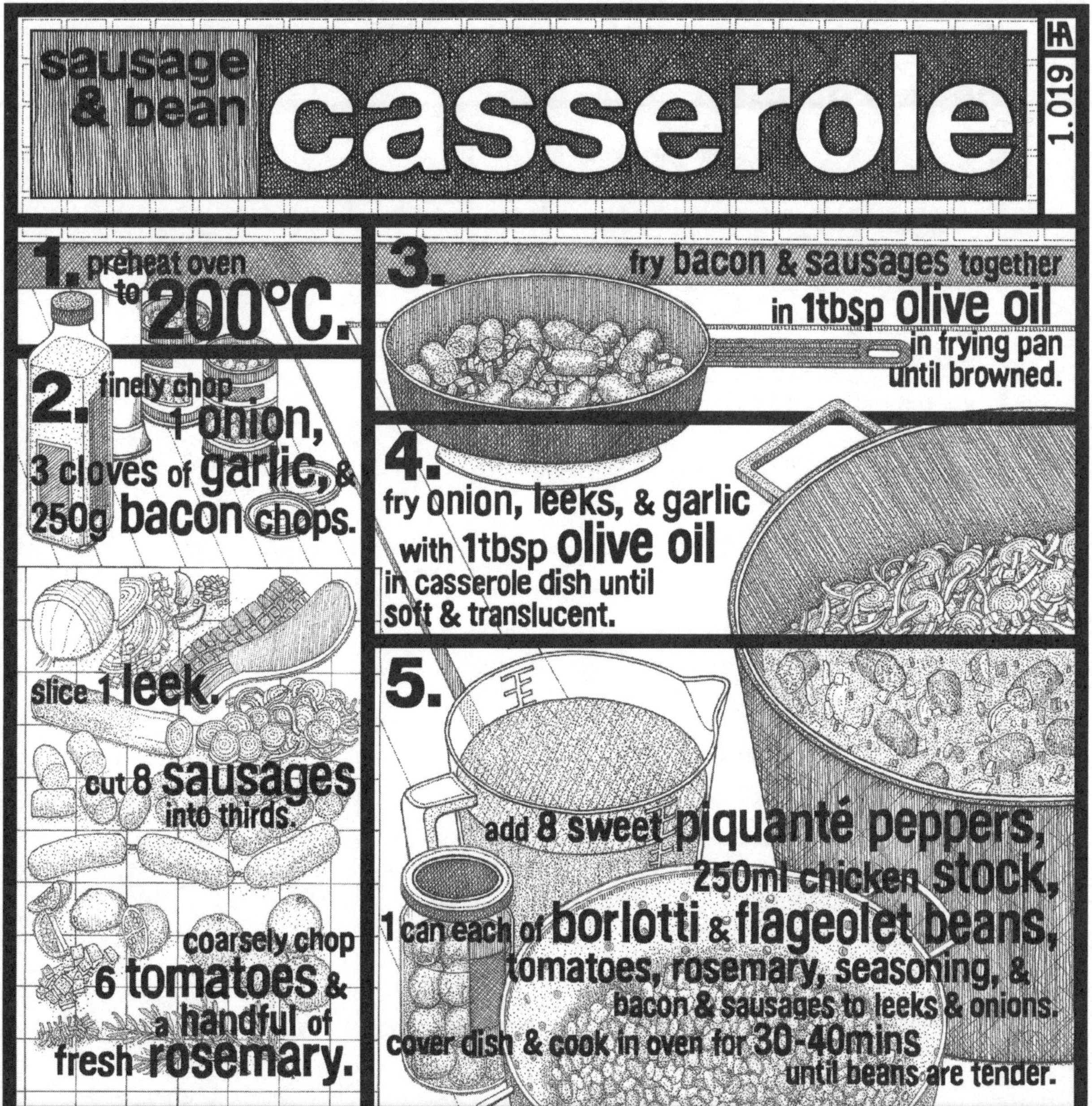
sausage & bean
casserole
1.019
1. preheat oven to 200°C.
2. finely chop 1 onion, 3 cloves of garlic, & 250g bacon chops.
slice 1 leek.
cut 8 sausages into thirds.
coarsely chop 6 tomatoes & a handful of fresh rosemary.
3. fry bacon & sausages together in 1tbsp olive oil in frying pan until browned.
4. fry onion, leeks, & garlic with 1tbsp olive oil in casserole dish until soft & translucent.
5. add 8 sweet piquanté peppers, 250ml chicken stock, 1 can each of borlotti & flageolet beans, tomatoes, rosemary, seasoning, & bacon & sausages to leeks & onions.
cover dish & cook in oven for 30-40mins until beans are tender.

shepherd's pie

1 large onion

2 carrots

1 leek

3 cloves of garlic

250g mushrooms

1kg potatoes

2tbsp olive oil

450g lean lamb mince

salt & pepper

3tsp fresh thyme

1tbsp plain flour

2tsp fresh oregano

200ml lamb stock

2tbsp butter

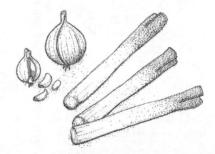

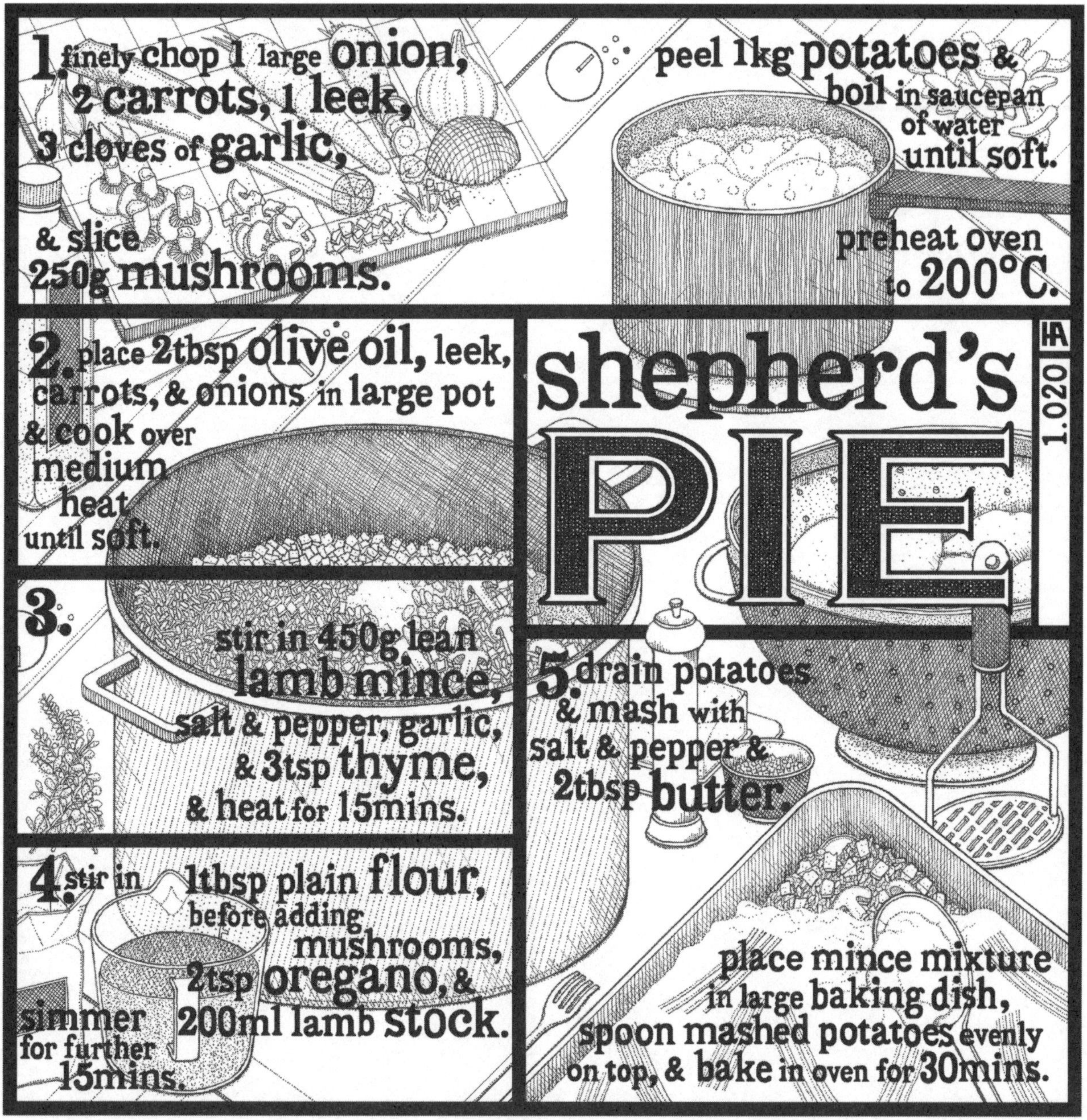
shepherd's PIE
1.020
1. finely chop 1 large onion, 2 carrots, 1 leek, 3 cloves of garlic,
& slice 250g mushrooms.
peel 1kg potatoes & boil in saucepan of water until soft.
preheat oven to 200°C.
2. place 2tbsp olive oil, leek, carrots, & onions in large pot & cook over medium heat until soft.
3. stir in 450g lean lamb mince, salt & pepper, garlic, & 3tsp thyme, & heat for 15mins.
4. stir in 1tbsp plain flour, before adding mushrooms, 2tsp oregano, & 200ml lamb stock.
simmer for further 15mins.
5. drain potatoes & mash with salt & pepper & 2tbsp butter.
place mince mixture in large baking dish, spoon mashed potatoes evenly on top, & bake in oven for 30mins.

crab cakes
fish in foil parcels
fish pie
fish stew
king prawn stir fry
tuna croquettes

main courses - fish

crab cakes

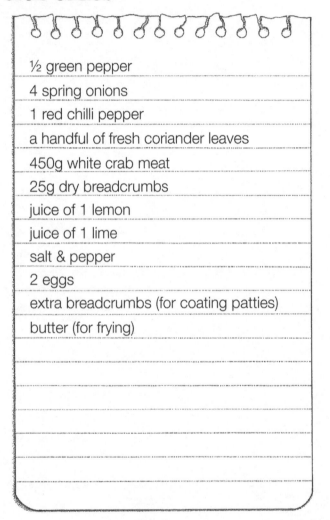

½ green pepper

4 spring onions

1 red chilli pepper

a handful of fresh coriander leaves

450g white crab meat

25g dry breadcrumbs

juice of 1 lemon

juice of 1 lime

salt & pepper

2 eggs

extra breadcrumbs (for coating patties)

butter (for frying)

great served with spicy salsa, french fries, & a mound of rocket leaves.

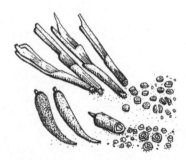

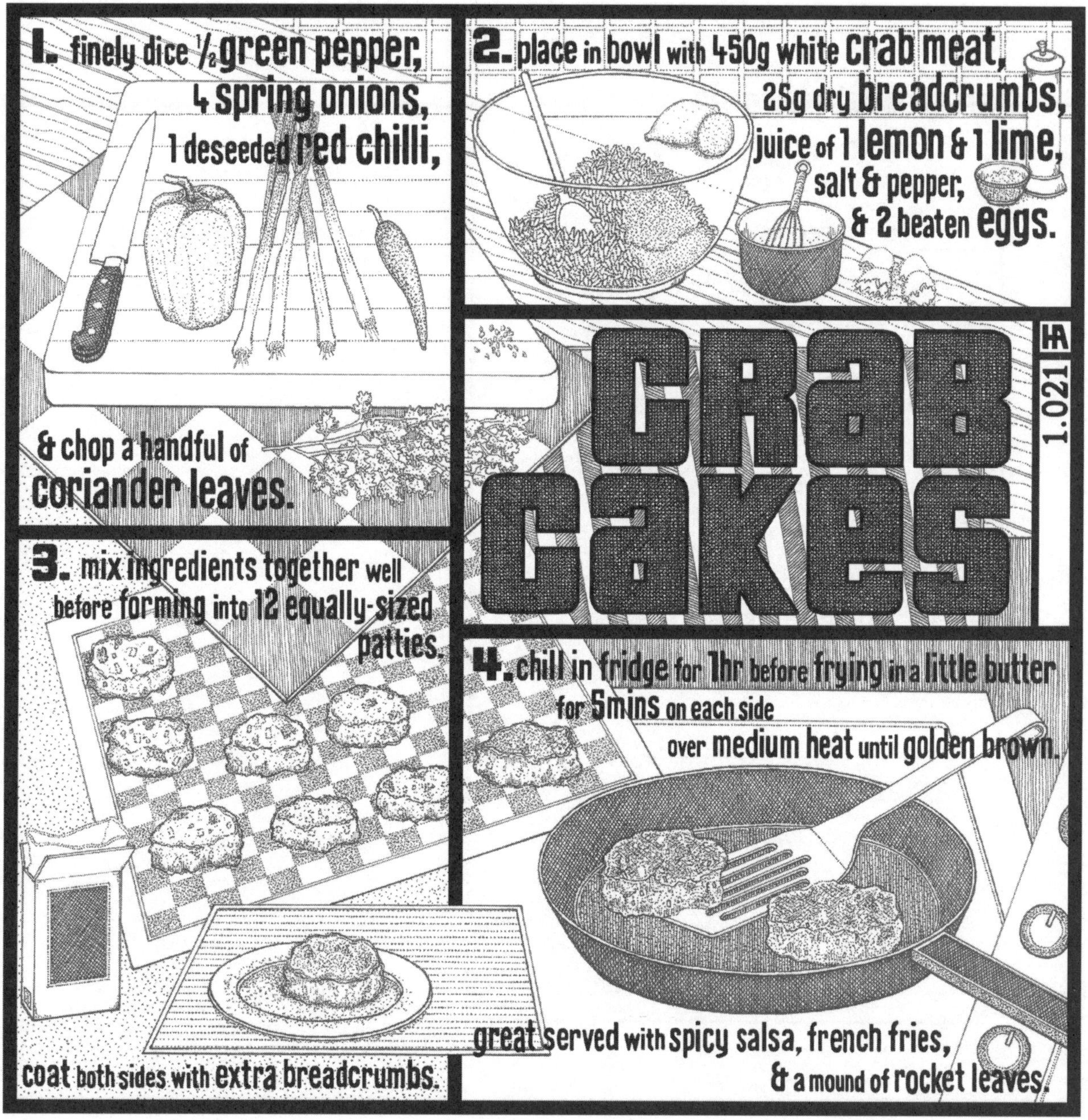
CRAB CAKES
HA
1.021
1. finely dice ½ green pepper,
4 spring onions,
1 deseeded red chilli,
& chop a handful of
coriander leaves.
2. place in bowl with 450g white crab meat,
25g dry breadcrumbs,
juice of 1 lemon & 1 lime,
salt & pepper,
& 2 beaten eggs.
3. mix ingredients together well
before forming into 12 equally-sized
patties.
coat both sides with extra breadcrumbs.
4. chill in fridge for 1hr before frying in a little butter
for 5mins on each side
over medium heat until golden brown.
great served with spicy salsa, french fries,
& a mound of rocket leaves.

fish in foil parcels

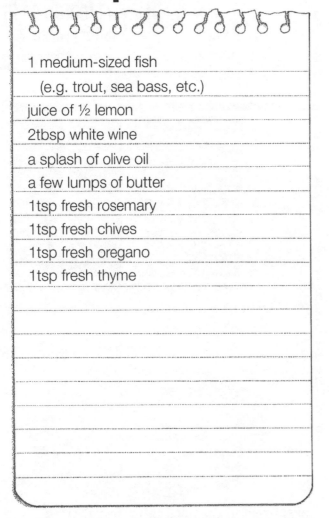

1 medium-sized fish
  (e.g. trout, sea bass, etc.)

juice of ½ lemon

2tbsp white wine

a splash of olive oil

a few lumps of butter

1tsp fresh rosemary

1tsp fresh chives

1tsp fresh oregano

1tsp fresh thyme

lime can be used as an alternative to lemon.

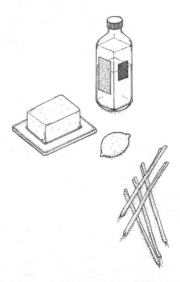

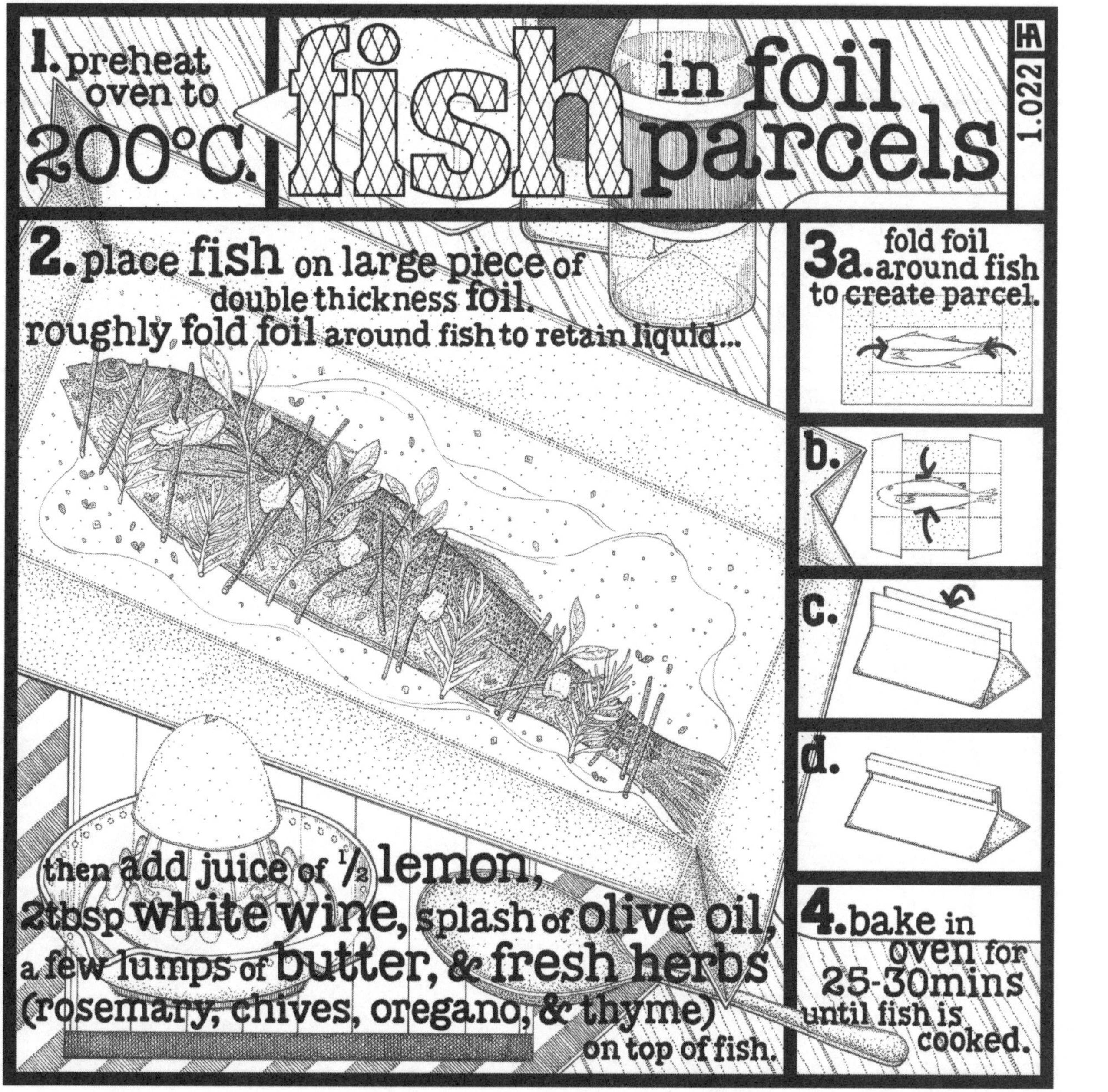
fish in foil parcels
HA
1.022
1. preheat oven to 200°C.
2. place fish on large piece of double thickness foil.
roughly fold foil around fish to retain liquid...
then add juice of ½ lemon,
2tbsp white wine, splash of olive oil,
a few lumps of butter, & fresh herbs
(rosemary, chives, oregano, & thyme)
on top of fish.
3a. fold foil around fish to create parcel.
b.
c.
d.
4. bake in oven for 25-30mins until fish is cooked.

fish pie

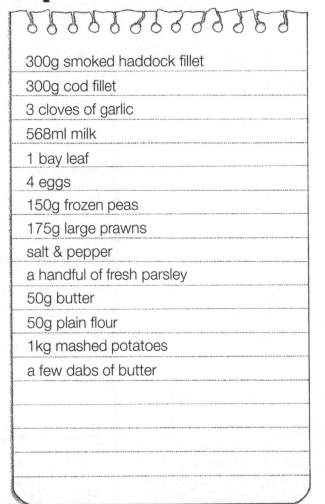

- 300g smoked haddock fillet
- 300g cod fillet
- 3 cloves of garlic
- 568ml milk
- 1 bay leaf
- 4 eggs
- 150g frozen peas
- 175g large prawns
- salt & pepper
- a handful of fresh parsley
- 50g butter
- 50g plain flour
- 1kg mashed potatoes
- a few dabs of butter

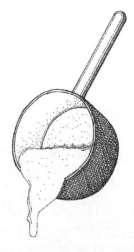

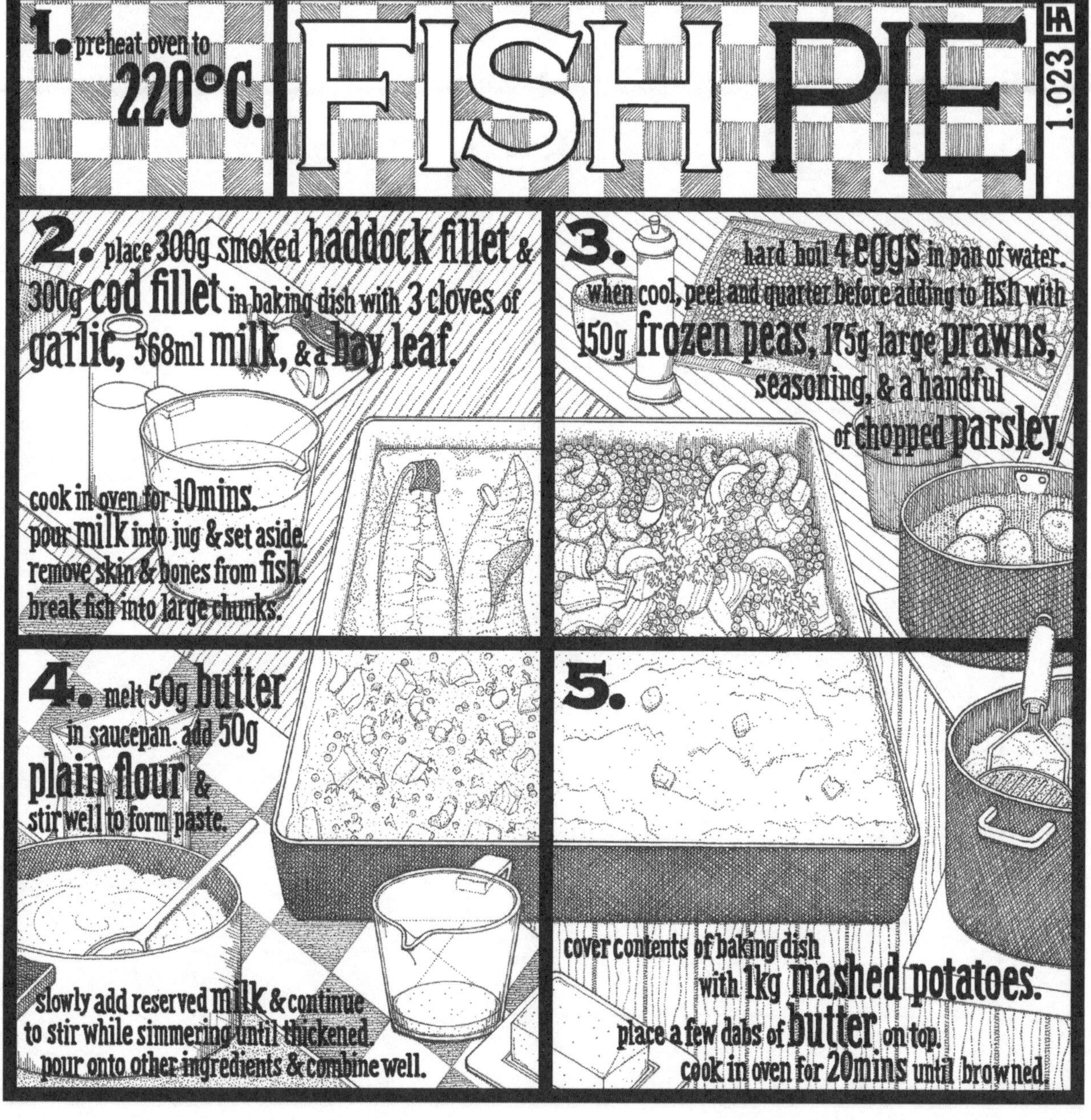
FISH PIE
HA
1.023
1. preheat oven to 220°C.
2. place 300g smoked haddock fillet & 300g cod fillet in baking dish with 3 cloves of garlic, 568ml milk, & a bay leaf.
cook in oven for 10mins. pour milk into jug & set aside. remove skin & bones from fish. break fish into large chunks.
3. hard boil 4 eggs in pan of water. when cool, peel and quarter before adding to fish with 150g frozen peas, 175g large prawns, seasoning, & a handful of chopped parsley.
4. melt 50g butter in saucepan. add 50g plain flour & stir well to form paste.
slowly add reserved milk & continue to stir while simmering until thickened. pour onto other ingredients & combine well.
5. cover contents of baking dish with 1kg mashed potatoes. place a few dabs of butter on top. cook in oven for 20mins until browned.

fish stew

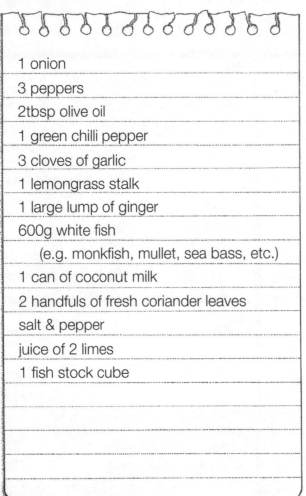

1 onion

3 peppers

2tbsp olive oil

1 green chilli pepper

3 cloves of garlic

1 lemongrass stalk

1 large lump of ginger

600g white fish
    (e.g. monkfish, mullet, sea bass, etc.)

1 can of coconut milk

2 handfuls of fresh coriander leaves

salt & pepper

juice of 2 limes

1 fish stock cube

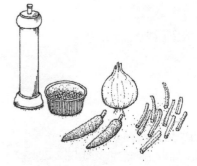

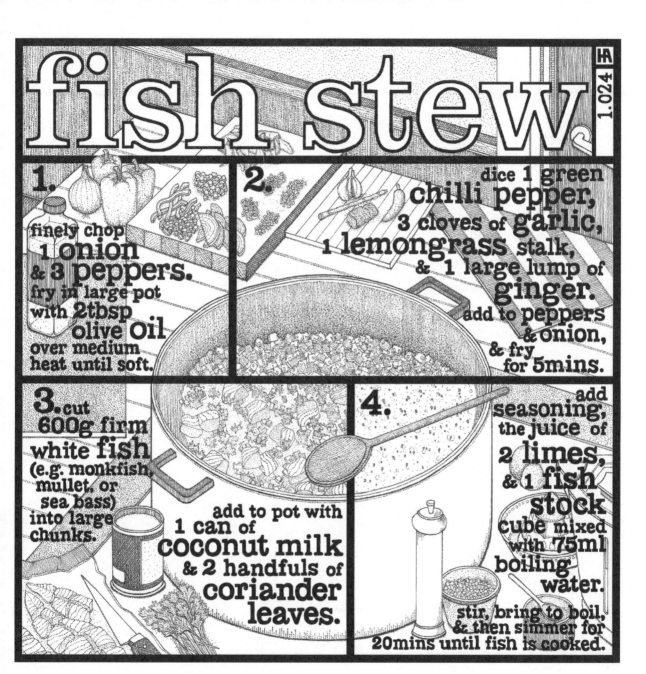

fish stew

1. finely chop **1 onion** & **3 peppers**. fry in large pot with **2tbsp olive oil** over medium heat until soft.

2. dice 1 green **chilli pepper,** 3 cloves of **garlic,** 1 **lemongrass** stalk, & 1 large lump of **ginger.** add to peppers & onion, & fry for **5mins**.

3. cut **600g firm white fish** (e.g. monkfish, mullet, or sea bass) into large chunks.

add to pot with **1 can of coconut milk** & 2 handfuls of **coriander leaves.**

4. add seasoning, the juice of **2 limes,** & **1 fish stock** cube mixed with **75ml boiling water.**

stir, bring to boil, & then simmer for 20mins until fish is cooked.

king prawn stir fry

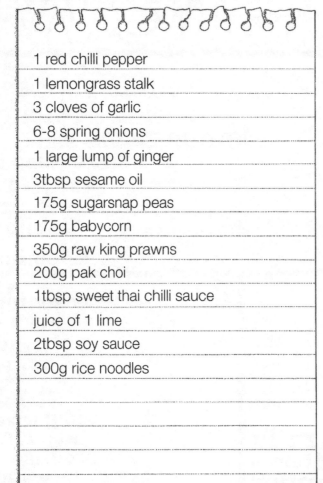

1 red chilli pepper

1 lemongrass stalk

3 cloves of garlic

6-8 spring onions

1 large lump of ginger

3tbsp sesame oil

175g sugarsnap peas

175g babycorn

350g raw king prawns

200g pak choi

1tbsp sweet thai chilli sauce

juice of 1 lime

2tbsp soy sauce

300g rice noodles

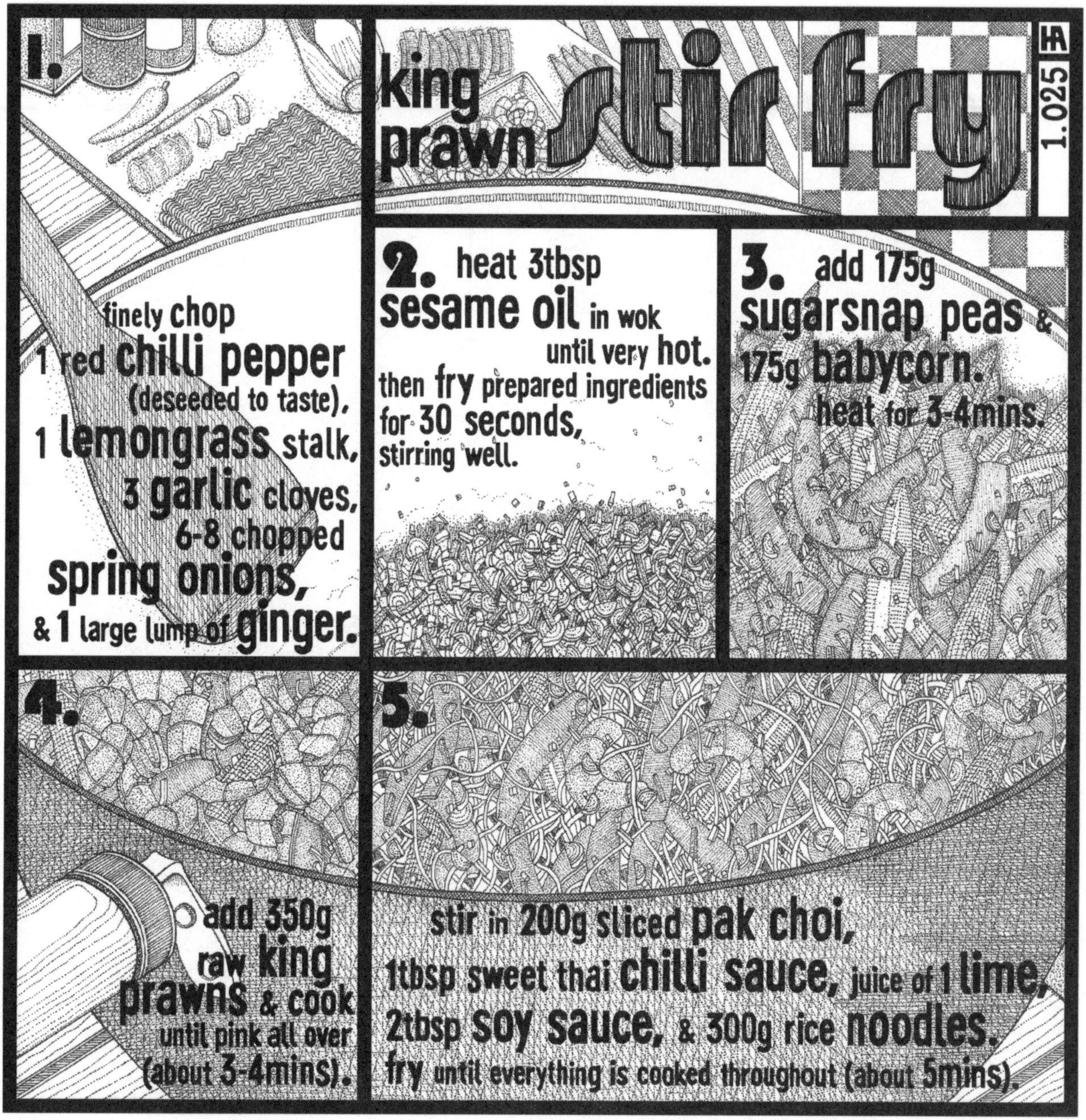
king prawn stir fry
1.025
1. finely chop
1 red chilli pepper
(deseeded to taste),
1 lemongrass stalk,
3 garlic cloves,
6-8 chopped
spring onions,
& 1 large lump of ginger.
2. heat 3tbsp
sesame oil in wok
until very hot.
then fry prepared ingredients
for 30 seconds,
stirring well.
3. add 175g
sugarsnap peas &
175g babycorn.
heat for 3-4mins.
4. add 350g
raw king
prawns & cook
until pink all over
(about 3-4mins).
5. stir in 200g sliced pak choi,
1tbsp sweet thai chilli sauce, juice of 1 lime,
2tbsp soy sauce, & 300g rice noodles.
fry until everything is cooked throughout (about 5mins).

tuna croquettes

serves 4

- 1 green chilli pepper
- 8 spring onions
- a handful of fresh coriander leaves
- 3 cans of tuna
- 1tbsp ground coriander
- salt & pepper
- 100g butter
- juice of 1 lemon
- zest of 1 & juice of 2 limes
- 2 eggs
- 100g breadcrumbs
- 1tbsp coriander seeds
- flour (for coating croquettes)
- sunflower oil (for frying)

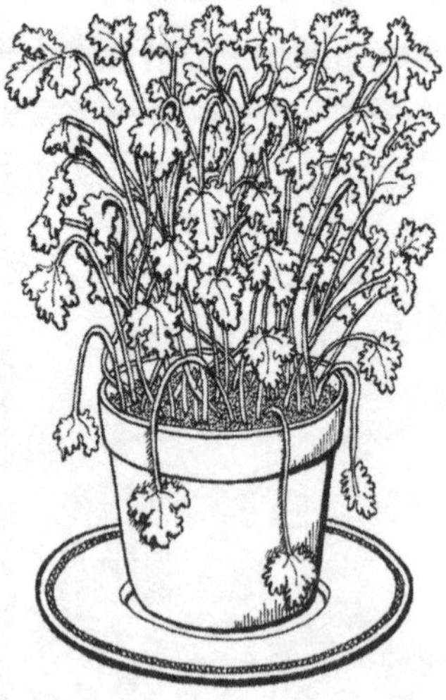

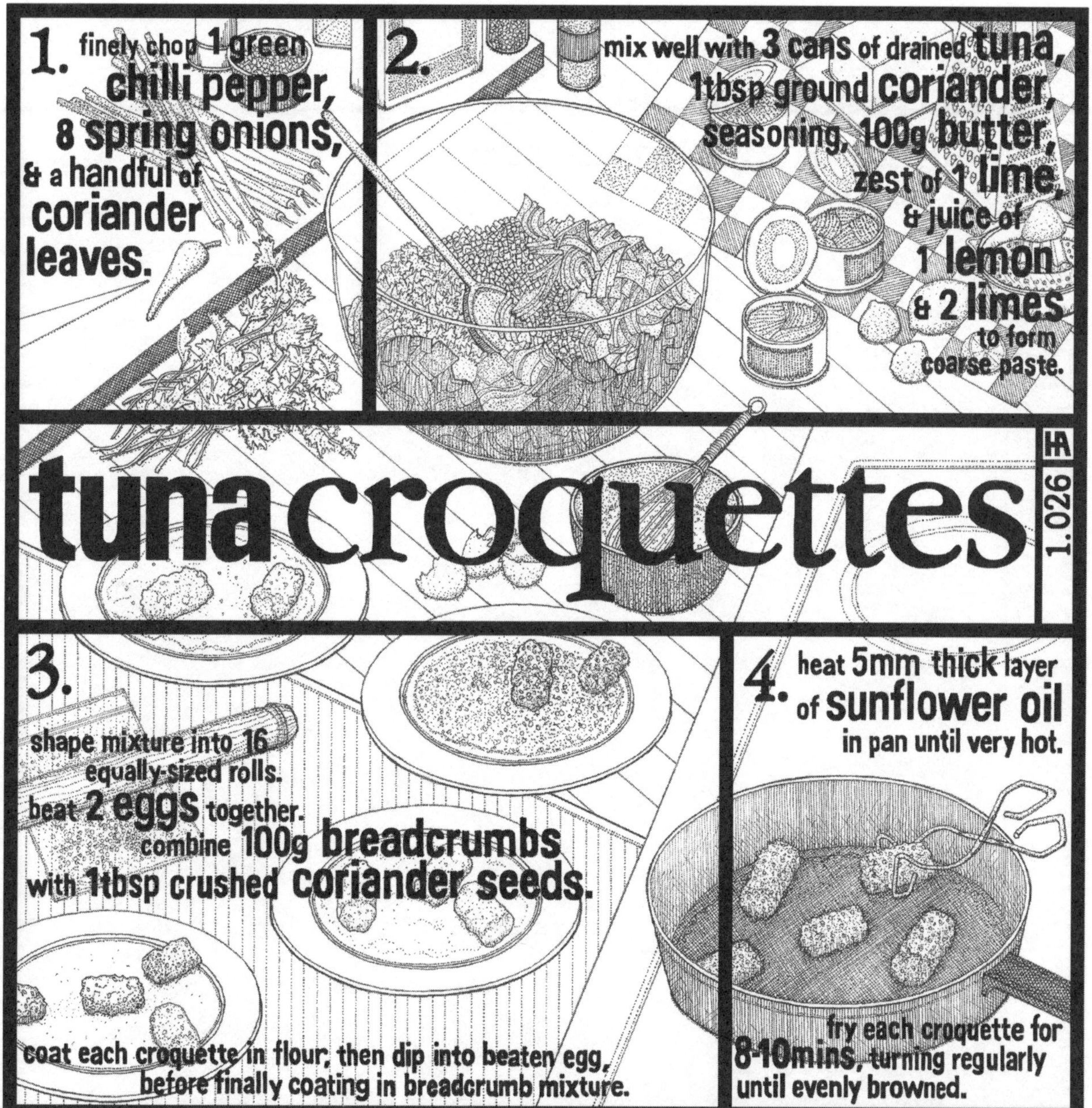
tuna croquettes
HA
1.026
1. finely chop 1 green chilli pepper, 8 spring onions, & a handful of coriander leaves.
2. mix well with 3 cans of drained tuna, 1tbsp ground coriander, seasoning, 100g butter, zest of 1 lime, & juice of 1 lemon & 2 limes to form coarse paste.
3. shape mixture into 16 equally-sized rolls.
beat 2 eggs together.
combine 100g breadcrumbs with 1tbsp crushed coriander seeds.
coat each croquette in flour, then dip into beaten egg, before finally coating in breadcrumb mixture.
4. heat 5mm thick layer of sunflower oil in pan until very hot.
fry each croquette for 8-10mins, turning regularly until evenly browned.

aduki bean burgers
pumpkin & chickpea curry
ratatouille
root vegetable tagine
spinach & mushroom pancakes
vegetable cottage pie

main courses - vegetarian

aduki bean burgers

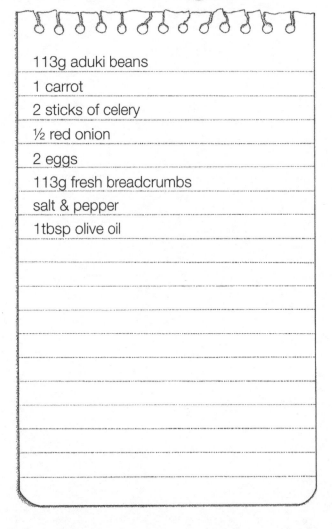

- 113g aduki beans
- 1 carrot
- 2 sticks of celery
- ½ red onion
- 2 eggs
- 113g fresh breadcrumbs
- salt & pepper
- 1tbsp olive oil

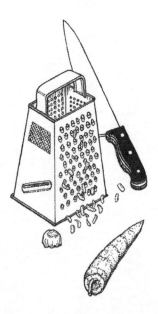

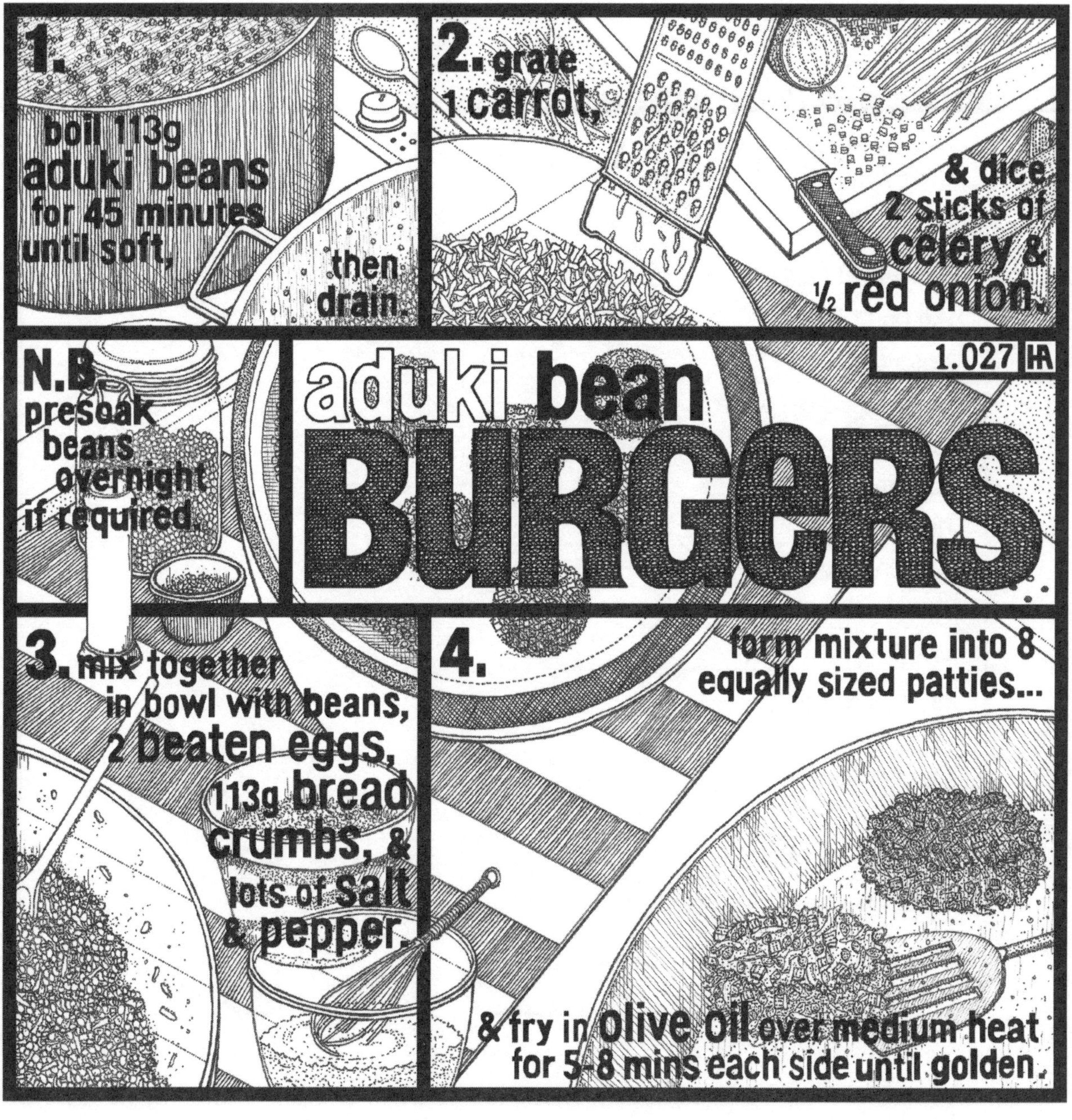

1.
boil 113g aduki beans for 45 minutes until soft,
then drain.
2. grate 1 carrot,
& dice 2 sticks of celery & ½ red onion.
N.B presoak beans overnight if required.
aduki bean BURGERS
1.027 HA
3. mix together in bowl with beans, 2 beaten eggs, 113g bread crumbs, & lots of salt & pepper.
4.
form mixture into 8 equally sized patties...
& fry in olive oil over medium heat for 5-8 mins each side until golden.

pumpkin & chickpea curry

1 onion

3 cloves of garlic

1kg pumpkin

1tbsp olive oil

2tsp ground coriander

2tsp cumin seeds

2tsp garam masala

1tsp turmeric

1tsp chilli powder

6 cardamom pods

juice of 1 lemon

500ml vegetable stock

salt & pepper

1 can of coconut milk

50g desiccated coconut

180g spinach leaves

2 cans of chickpeas (drained)

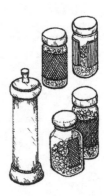

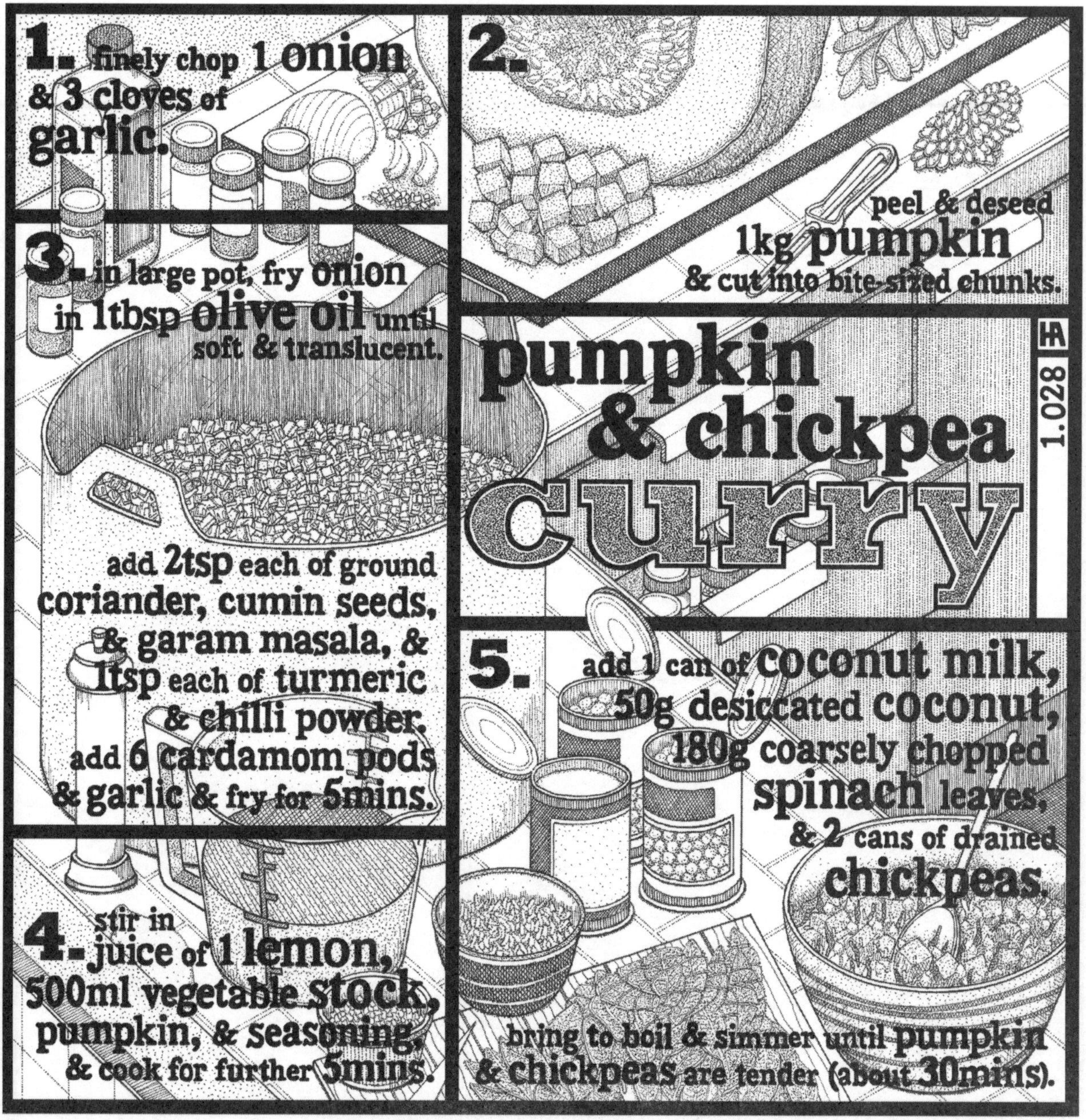
1. finely chop 1 onion & 3 cloves of garlic.
2. peel & deseed 1kg pumpkin & cut into bite-sized chunks.
3. in large pot, fry onion in 1tbsp olive oil until soft & translucent.
add 2tsp each of ground coriander, cumin seeds, & garam masala, & 1tsp each of turmeric & chilli powder.
add 6 cardamom pods & garlic & fry for 5mins.
pumpkin & chickpea curry
HA
1.028
4. stir in juice of 1 lemon, 500ml vegetable stock, pumpkin, & seasoning, & cook for further 5mins.
5. add 1 can of coconut milk, 50g desiccated coconut, 180g coarsely chopped spinach leaves, & 2 cans of drained chickpeas.
bring to boil & simmer until pumpkin & chickpeas are tender (about 30mins).

ratatouille

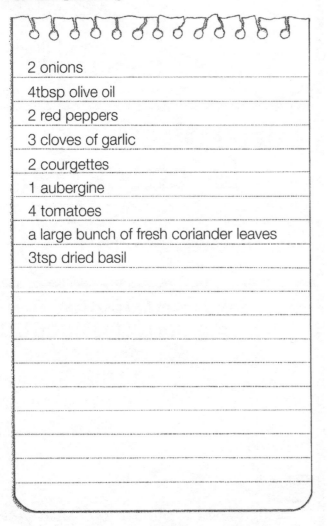

2 onions

4tbsp olive oil

2 red peppers

3 cloves of garlic

2 courgettes

1 aubergine

4 tomatoes

a large bunch of fresh coriander leaves

3tsp dried basil

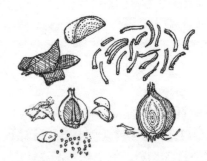

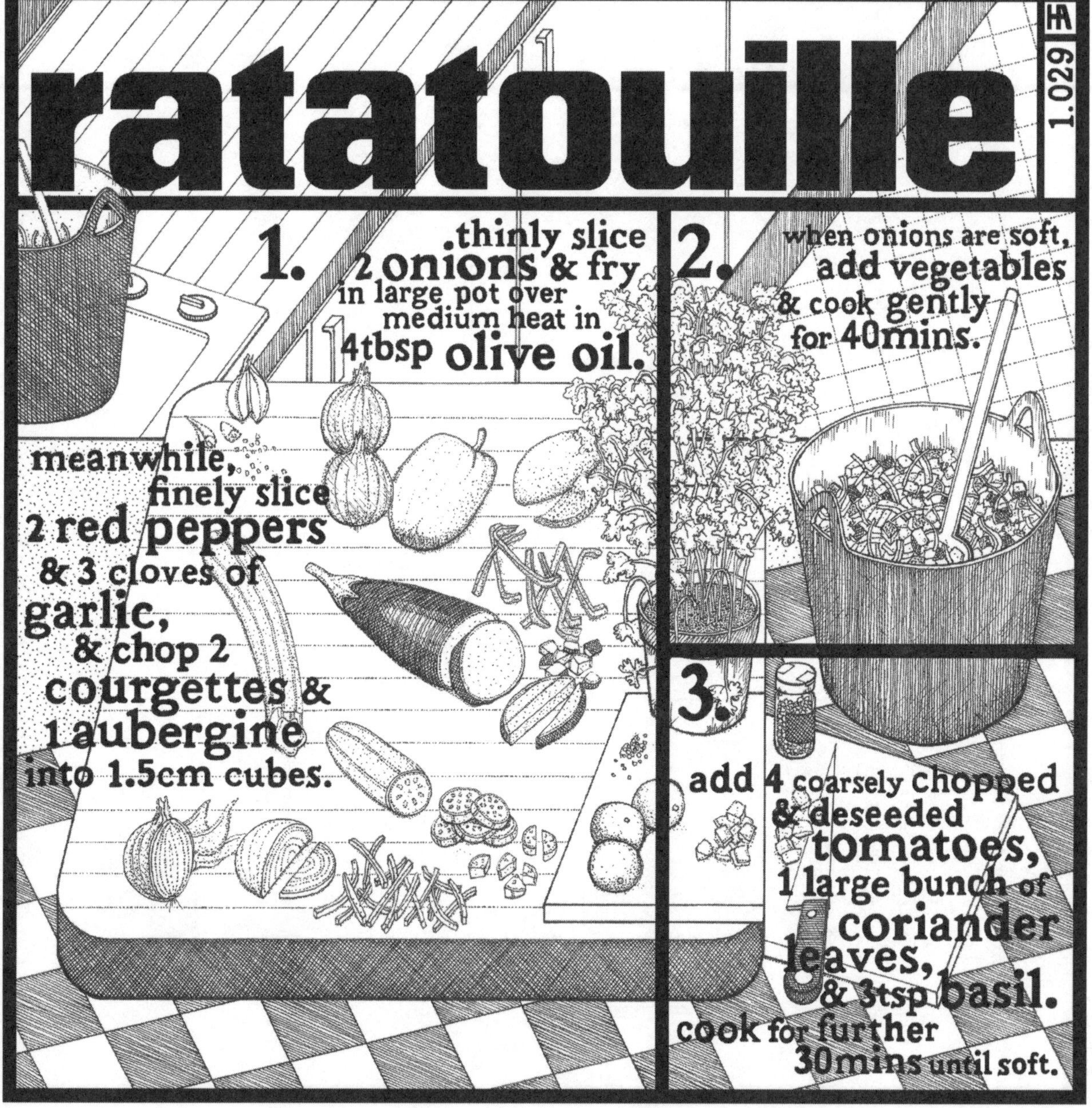
ratatouille
1.029
1. thinly slice 2 onions & fry in large pot over medium heat in 4tbsp olive oil.
meanwhile, finely slice 2 red peppers & 3 cloves of garlic, & chop 2 courgettes & 1 aubergine into 1.5cm cubes.
2. when onions are soft, add vegetables & cook gently for 40mins.
3. add 4 coarsely chopped & deseeded tomatoes, 1 large bunch of coriander leaves, & 3tsp basil. cook for further 30mins until soft.

root vegetable tagine

serves 4-6

- 1 red onion
- 3 cloves of garlic
- 2 carrots
- 1 parsnip
- 1 swede
- 120g dried apricots
- 100g blanched almonds
- 1 sweet potato
- 1tsp ground ginger
- 1tsp ground cinnamon
- 1tsp turmeric
- 1tsp cayenne pepper
- 2tsp cumin seeds
- 500ml vegetable stock
- 2tsp olive oil
- salt & pepper
- a handful of fresh coriander leaves
- a handful of fresh parsley leaves

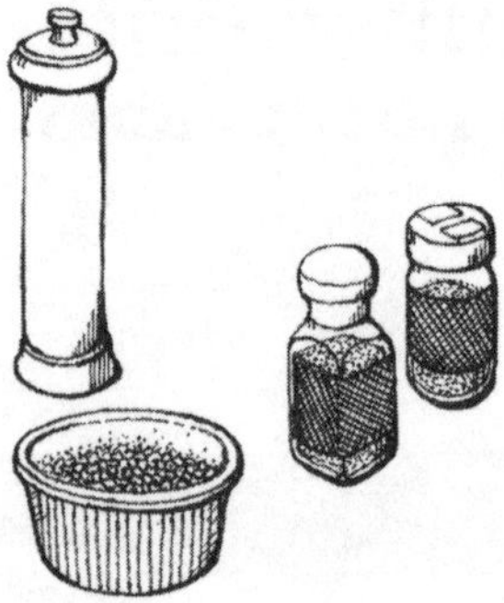

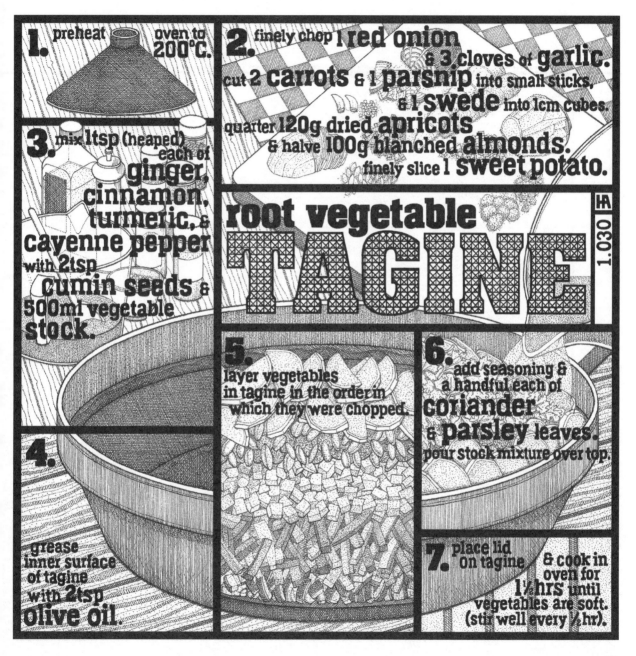

1. preheat oven to 200°C.

2. finely chop 1 **red onion** & 3 cloves of **garlic**. cut 2 **carrots** & 1 **parsnip** into small sticks, & 1 **swede** into 1cm cubes. quarter 120g dried **apricots** & halve 100g blanched **almonds**. finely slice 1 **sweet potato**.

3. mix 1tsp (heaped) each of **ginger, cinnamon, turmeric,** & **cayenne pepper** with 2tsp **cumin seeds** & 500ml vegetable **stock**.

root vegetable TAGINE

1.030

4. grease inner surface of tagine with **2tsp olive oil**.

5. layer vegetables in tagine in the order in which they were chopped.

6. add seasoning & a handful each of **coriander** & **parsley** leaves. pour stock mixture over top.

7. place lid on tagine & cook in oven for 1½hrs until vegetables are soft. (stir well every ½hr).

spinach & mushroom pancakes

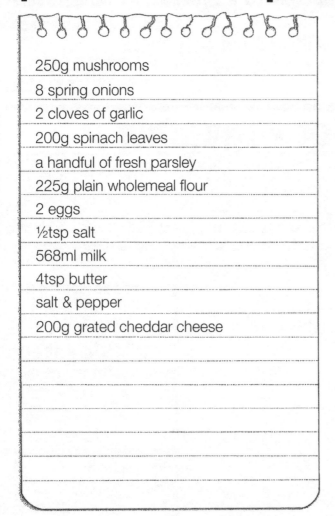

- 250g mushrooms
- 8 spring onions
- 2 cloves of garlic
- 200g spinach leaves
- a handful of fresh parsley
- 225g plain wholemeal flour
- 2 eggs
- ½tsp salt
- 568ml milk
- 4tsp butter
- salt & pepper
- 200g grated cheddar cheese

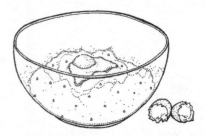

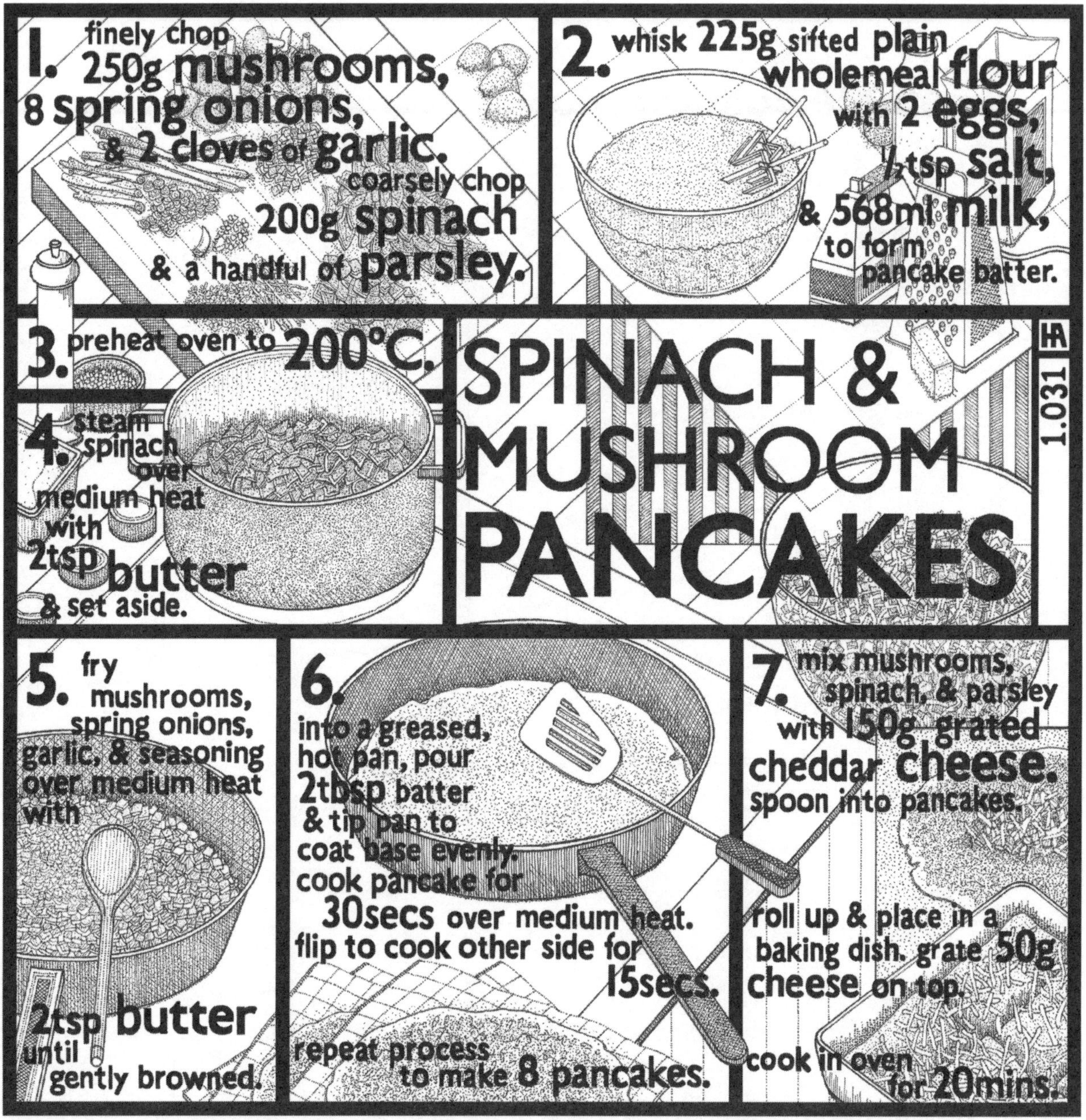
1. finely chop 250g mushrooms, 8 spring onions, & 2 cloves of garlic.
coarsely chop 200g spinach & a handful of parsley.
2. whisk 225g sifted plain wholemeal flour with 2 eggs, ½tsp salt, & 568ml milk, to form pancake batter.
3. preheat oven to 200°C.
SPINACH & MUSHROOM PANCAKES
1.031
4. steam spinach over medium heat with 2tsp butter & set aside.
5. fry mushrooms, spring onions, garlic, & seasoning over medium heat with 2tsp butter until gently browned.
6. into a greased, hot pan, pour 2tbsp batter & tip pan to coat base evenly. cook pancake for 30secs over medium heat. flip to cook other side for 15secs.
repeat process to make 8 pancakes.
7. mix mushrooms, spinach, & parsley with 150g grated cheddar cheese. spoon into pancakes.
roll up & place in a baking dish. grate 50g cheese on top.
cook in oven for 20mins.

vegetable cottage pie

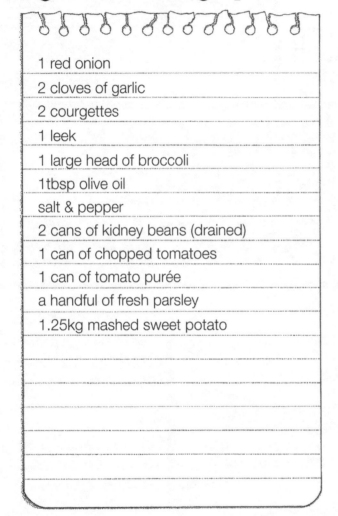

1 red onion

2 cloves of garlic

2 courgettes

1 leek

1 large head of broccoli

1tbsp olive oil

salt & pepper

2 cans of kidney beans (drained)

1 can of chopped tomatoes

1 can of tomato purée

a handful of fresh parsley

1.25kg mashed sweet potato

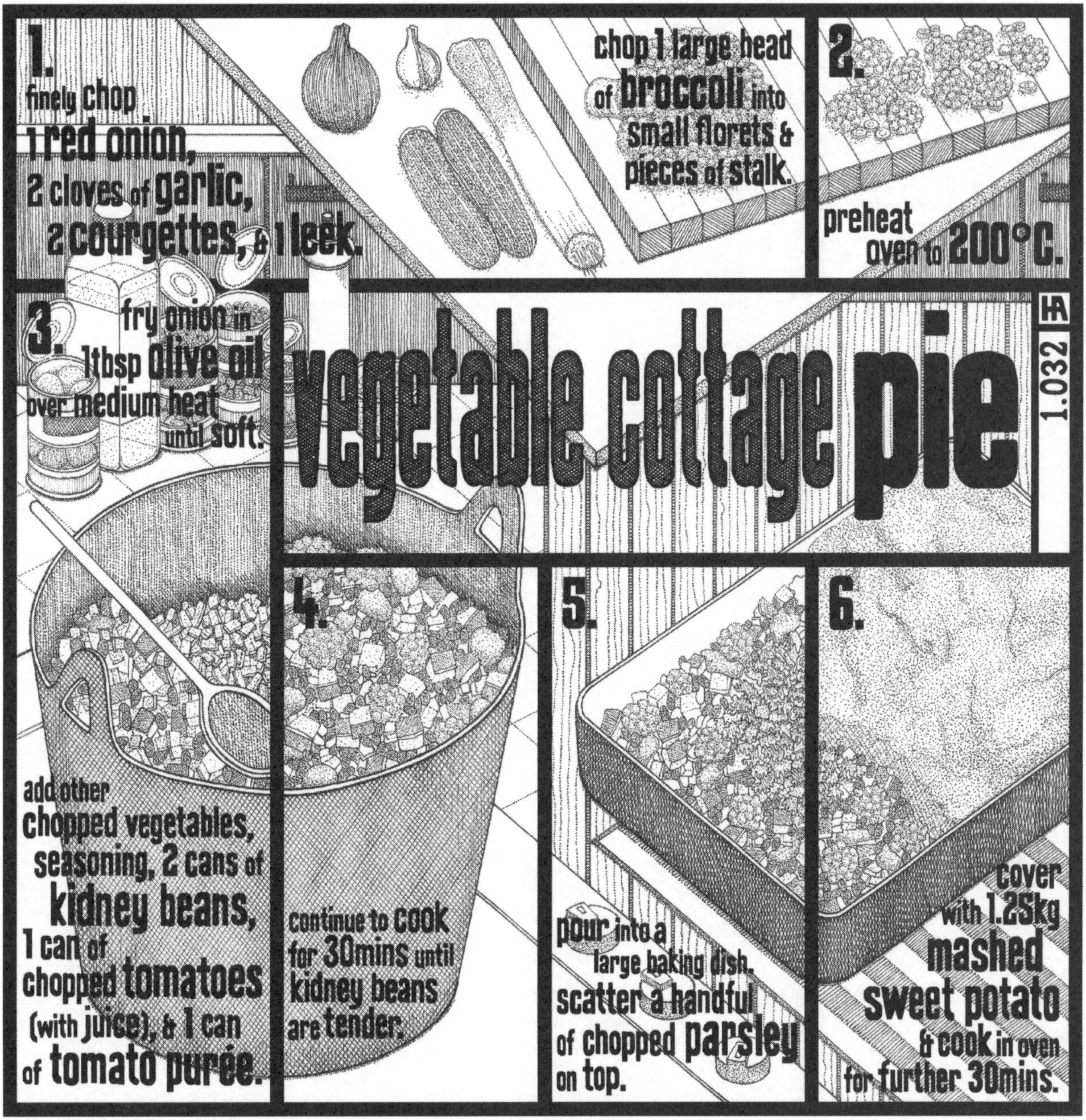
vegetable cottage pie
1.032
1. finely chop 1 red onion, 2 cloves of garlic, 2 courgettes, & 1 leek.
chop 1 large head of broccoli into small florets & pieces of stalk.
2. preheat oven to 200°C.
3. fry onion in 1tbsp olive oil over medium heat until soft.
add other chopped vegetables, seasoning, 2 cans of kidney beans, 1 can of chopped tomatoes (with juice), & 1 can of tomato purée.
4. continue to cook for 30mins until kidney beans are tender.
5. pour into a large baking dish. scatter a handful of chopped parsley on top.
6. cover with 1.25kg mashed sweet potato & cook in oven for further 30mins.

braised cabbage
cauliflower cheese
egg muffins
potato cakes
rösti potatoes
stuffed peppers

vegetables & side dishes

braised cabbage

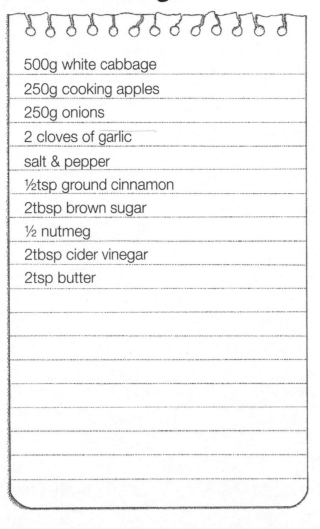

500g white cabbage

250g cooking apples

250g onions

2 cloves of garlic

salt & pepper

½tsp ground cinnamon

2tbsp brown sugar

½ nutmeg

2tbsp cider vinegar

2tsp butter

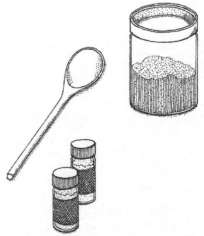

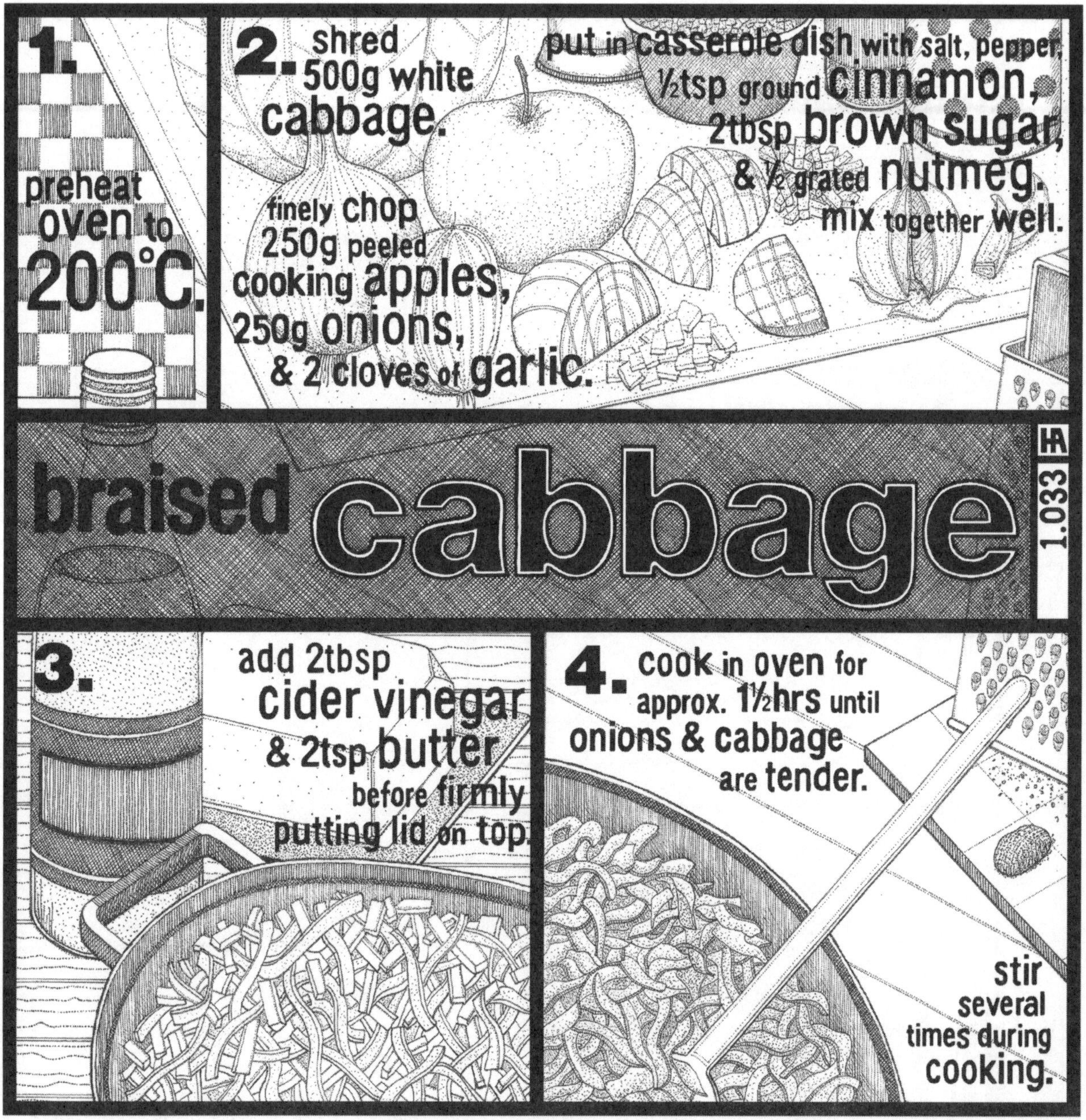
1.
preheat oven to 200°C.
2.
shred 500g white cabbage.
finely chop 250g peeled cooking apples, 250g onions, & 2 cloves of garlic.
put in casserole dish with salt, pepper, ½tsp ground cinnamon, 2tbsp brown sugar, & ½ grated nutmeg.
mix together well.
braised cabbage
HA
1.033
3.
add 2tbsp cider vinegar & 2tsp butter before firmly putting lid on top.
4.
cook in oven for approx. 1½hrs until onions & cabbage are tender.
stir several times during cooking.

cauliflower cheese

serves 4-6

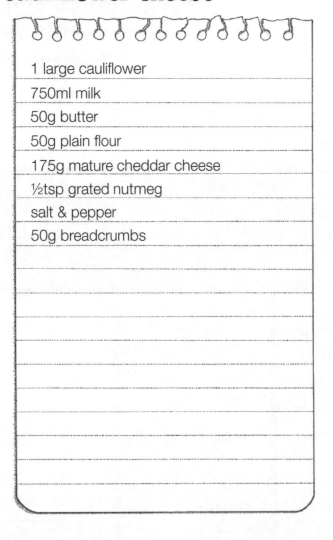

1 large cauliflower

750ml milk

50g butter

50g plain flour

175g mature cheddar cheese

½tsp grated nutmeg

salt & pepper

50g breadcrumbs

**also good with
1 or 2 finely chopped
cloves of garlic.**

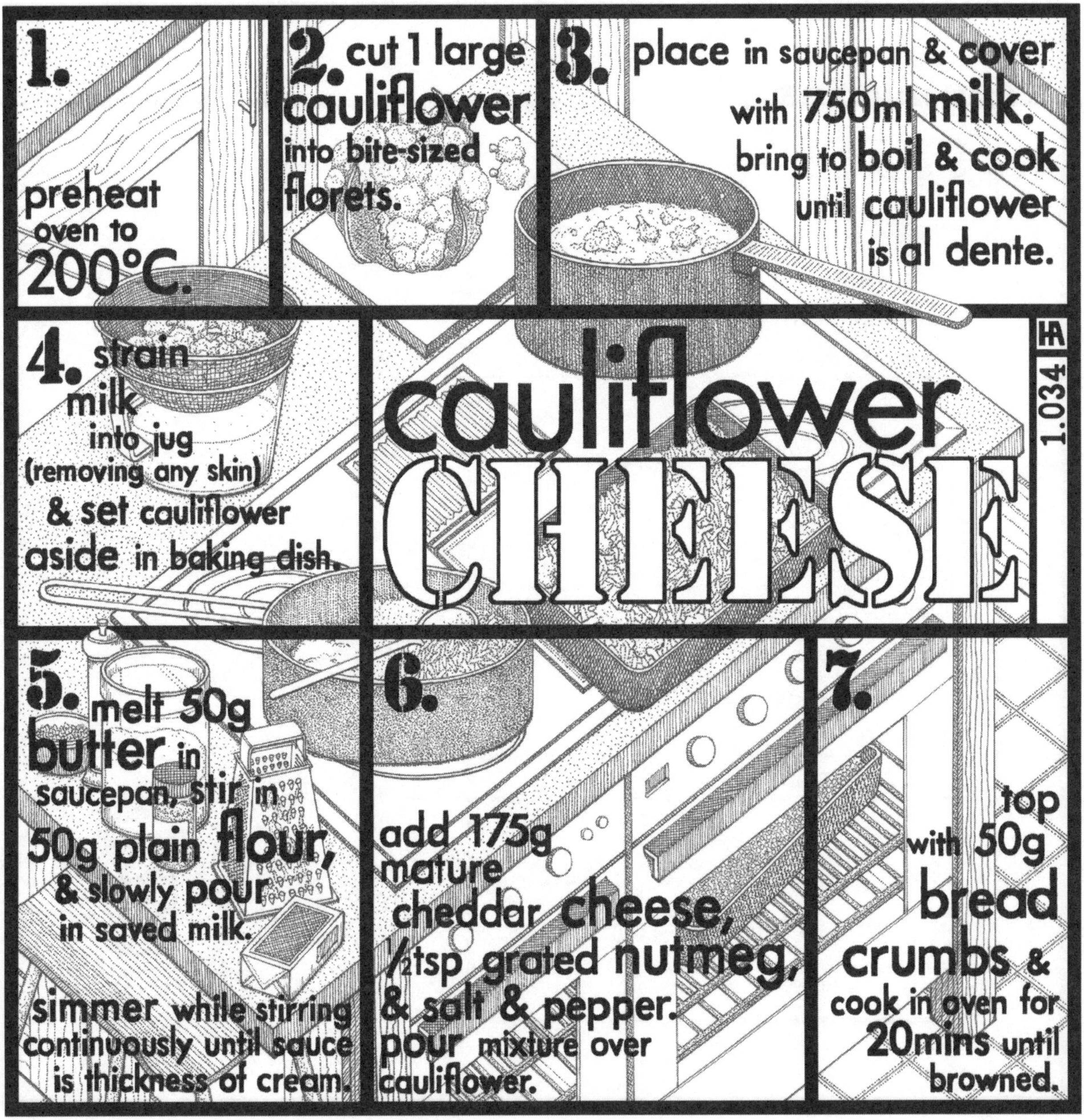
cauliflower
CHEESE
HA
1.034
1. preheat oven to 200°C.
2. cut 1 large cauliflower into bite-sized florets.
3. place in saucepan & cover with 750ml milk. bring to boil & cook until cauliflower is al dente.
4. strain milk into jug (removing any skin) & set cauliflower aside in baking dish.
5. melt 50g butter in saucepan, stir in 50g plain flour, & slowly pour in saved milk.
simmer while stirring continuously until sauce is thickness of cream.
6.
add 175g mature cheddar cheese, ½tsp grated nutmeg, & salt & pepper.
pour mixture over cauliflower.
7.
top with 50g bread crumbs & cook in oven for 20mins until browned.

egg muffins

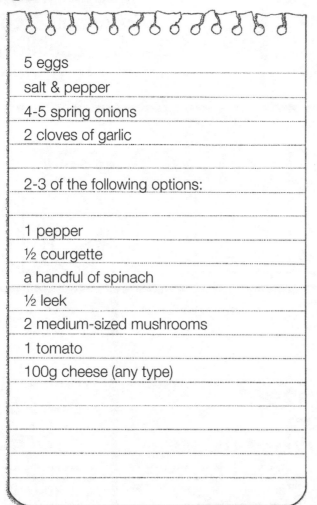

5 eggs

salt & pepper

4-5 spring onions

2 cloves of garlic

2-3 of the following options:

1 pepper

½ courgette

a handful of spinach

½ leek

2 medium-sized mushrooms

1 tomato

100g cheese (any type)

egg muffins

1. preheat oven to **190°C.**

2. finely chop **2-3** of the following options:
a) ½ leek
b) ½ courgette
c) a handful of spinach
d) 1 pepper
e) 2 medium-sized mushrooms
f) 1 tomato
g) 100g cheese

3. divide the chopped ingredients equally between 6 compartments in a greased muffin tin.

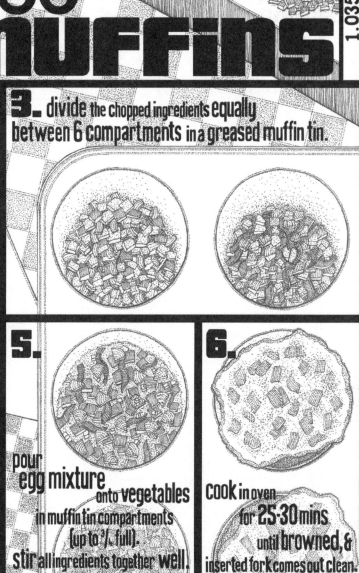

4. in a jug beat 5 eggs... adding salt & pepper, **4-5** finely chopped spring onions, & **2** diced cloves of garlic.

5. pour egg mixture onto vegetables in muffin tin compartments (up to ¾ full). stir all ingredients together well.

6. cook in oven for **25-30 mins** until browned, & inserted fork comes out clean.

potato cakes

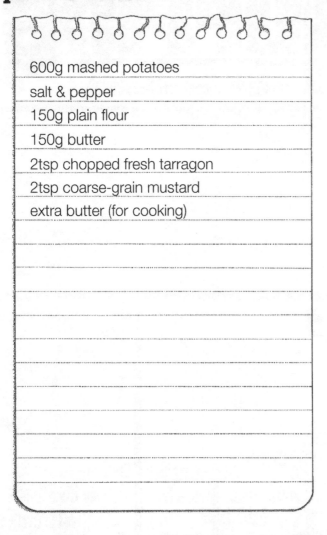

600g mashed potatoes

salt & pepper

150g plain flour

150g butter

2tsp chopped fresh tarragon

2tsp coarse-grain mustard

extra butter (for cooking)

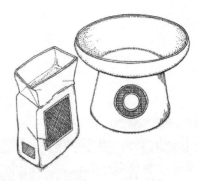

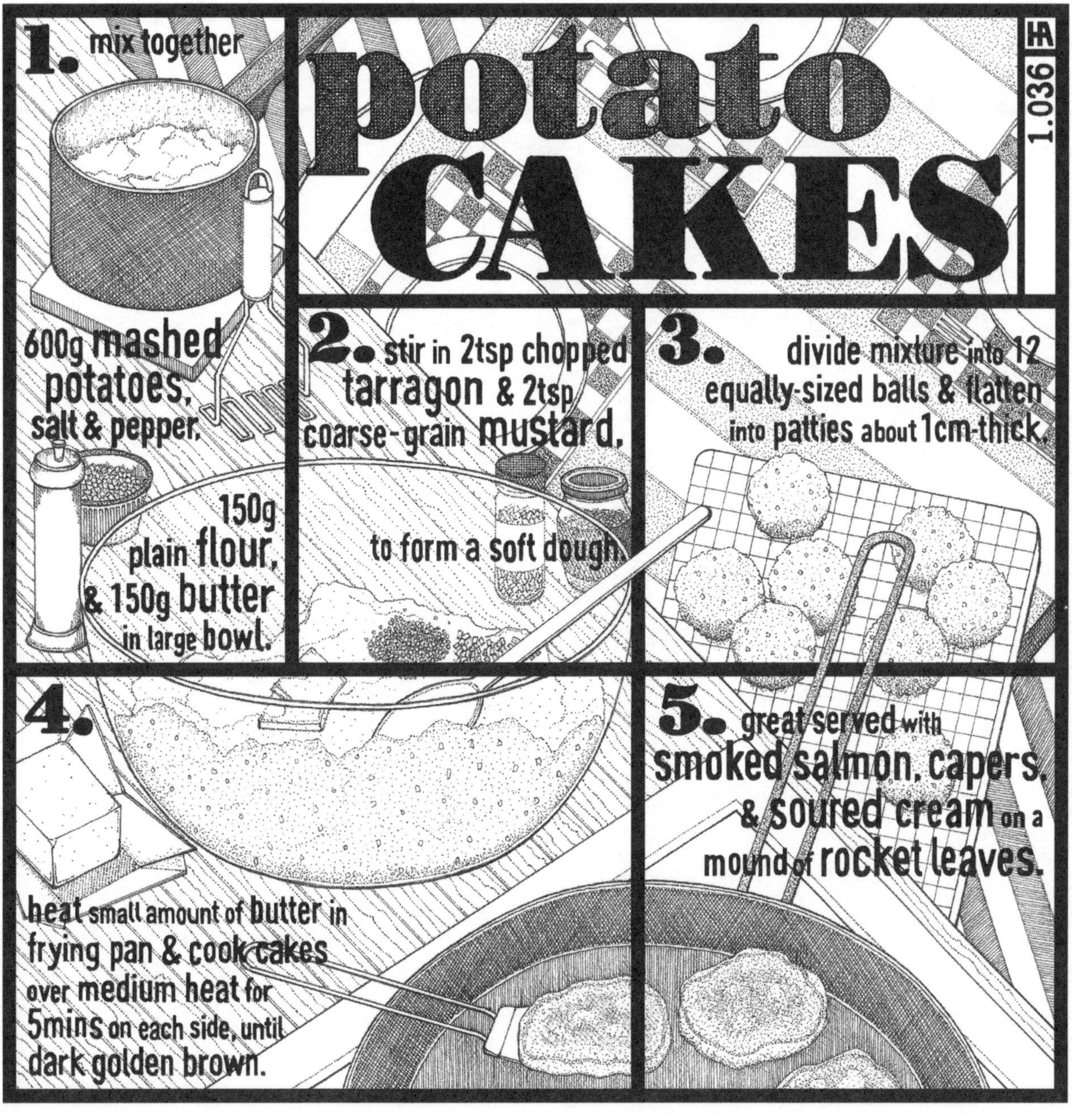

potato
CAKES
HA
1.036
1. mix together
600g mashed potatoes, salt & pepper,
150g plain flour, & 150g butter in large bowl.
2. stir in 2tsp chopped tarragon & 2tsp coarse-grain mustard,
to form a soft dough.
3. divide mixture into 12 equally-sized balls & flatten into patties about 1cm-thick.
4.
heat small amount of butter in frying pan & cook cakes over medium heat for 5mins on each side, until dark golden brown.
5. great served with smoked salmon, capers, & soured cream on a mound of rocket leaves.

rösti potatoes

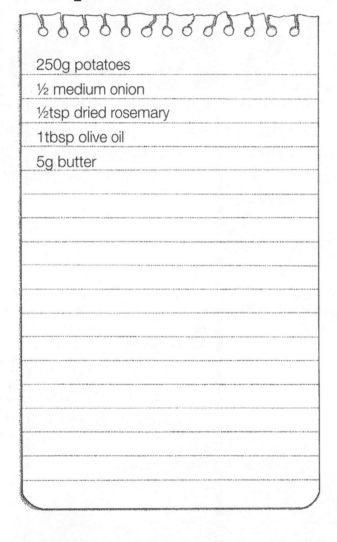

250g potatoes

½ medium onion

½tsp dried rosemary

1tbsp olive oil

5g butter

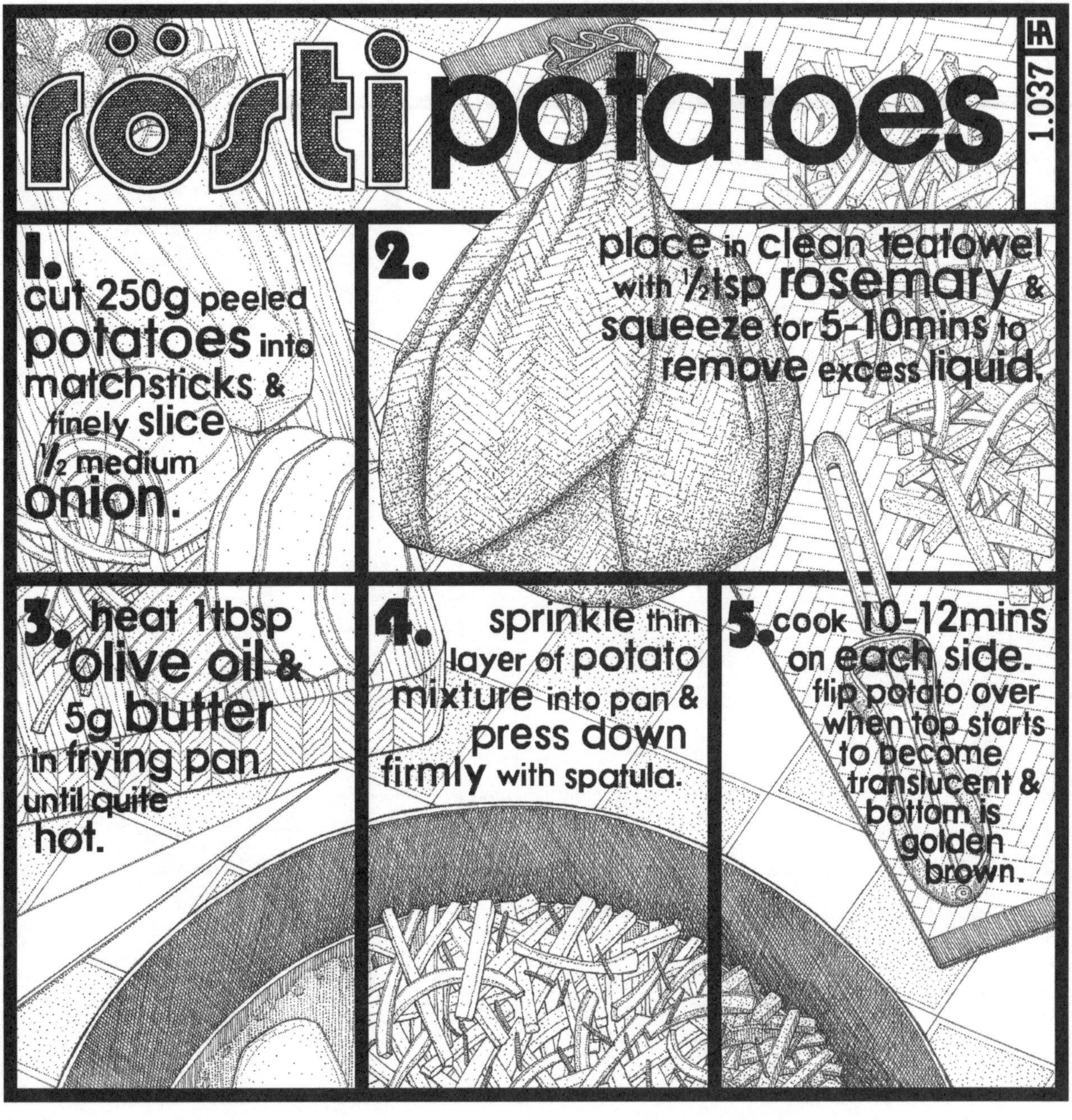

röstipotatoes
HA
1.037
1. cut 250g peeled potatoes into matchsticks & finely slice ½ medium onion.
2. place in clean teatowel with ½tsp rosemary & squeeze for 5-10mins to remove excess liquid.
3. heat 1tbsp olive oil & 5g butter in frying pan until quite hot.
4. sprinkle thin layer of potato mixture into pan & press down firmly with spatula.
5. cook 10-12mins on each side. flip potato over when top starts to become translucent & bottom is golden brown.

stuffed peppers

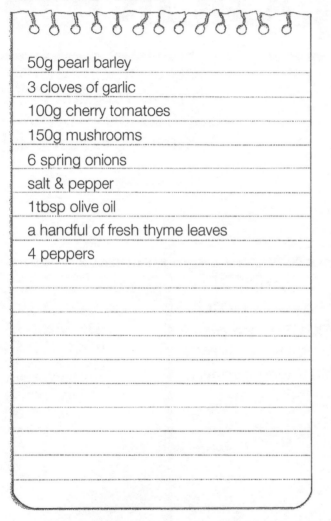

50g pearl barley

3 cloves of garlic

100g cherry tomatoes

150g mushrooms

6 spring onions

salt & pepper

1tbsp olive oil

a handful of fresh thyme leaves

4 peppers

couscous or rice can be used as an alternative to pearl barley.

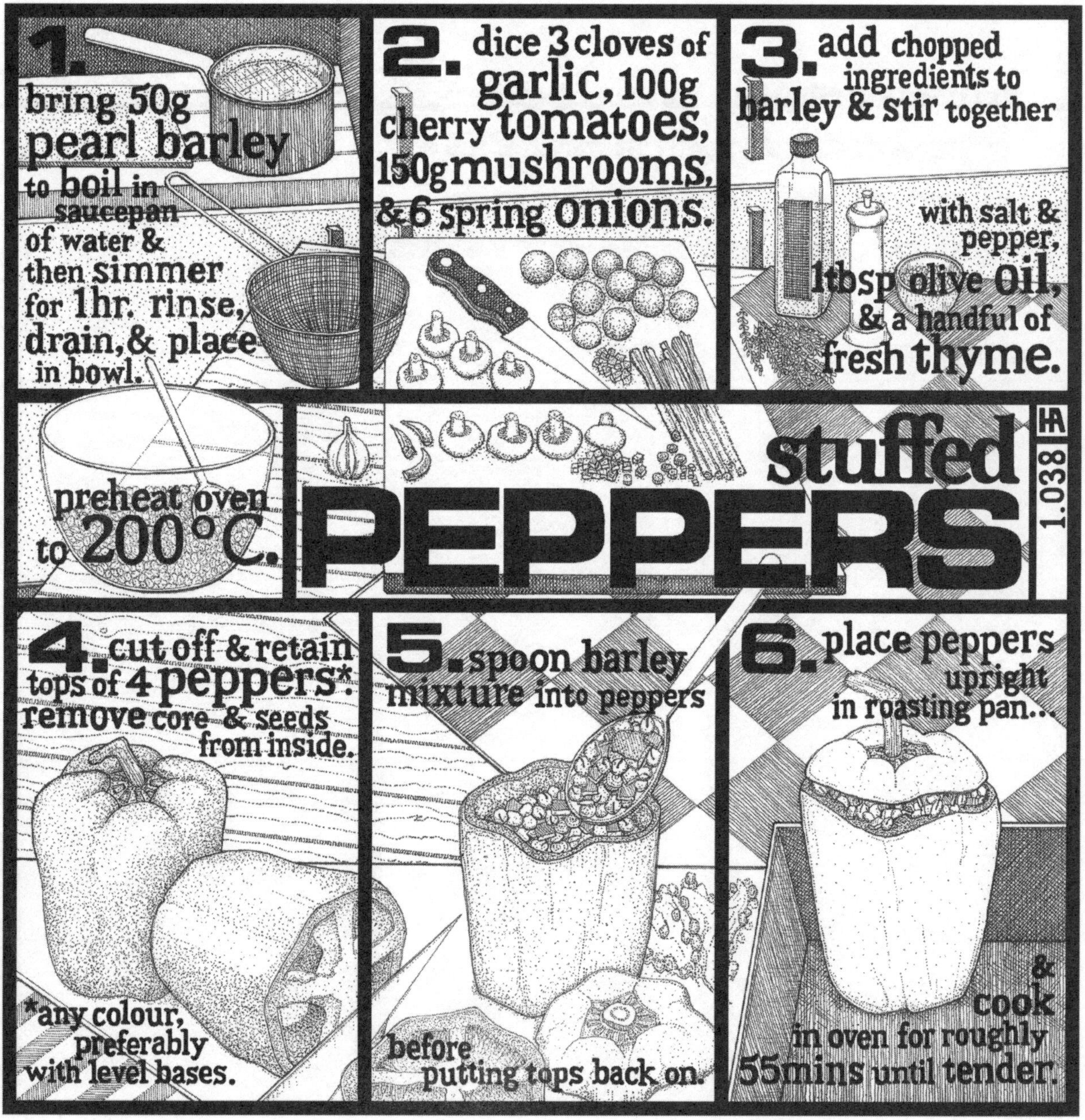
stuffed PEPPERS
1.038
HA
1. bring 50g pearl barley to boil in saucepan of water & then simmer for 1hr. rinse, drain, & place in bowl.
2. dice 3 cloves of garlic, 100g cherry tomatoes, 150g mushrooms, & 6 spring onions.
3. add chopped ingredients to barley & stir together
with salt & pepper, 1tbsp olive oil, & a handful of fresh thyme.
preheat oven to 200°C.
4. cut off & retain tops of 4 peppers*. remove core & seeds from inside.
*any colour, preferably with level bases.
5. spoon barley mixture into peppers
before putting tops back on.
6. place peppers upright in roasting pan...
& cook in oven for roughly 55mins until tender.

bread & butter pudding
chocolate soufflé
crème anglaise
gooseberry crumble
île flottante
rhubarb fool
rice pudding
syllabub

puddings

bread & butter pudding serves 4

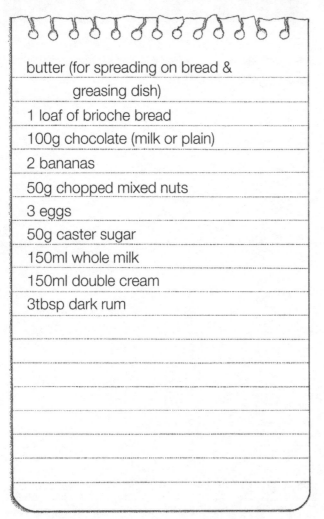

butter (for spreading on bread &
    greasing dish)

1 loaf of brioche bread

100g chocolate (milk or plain)

2 bananas

50g chopped mixed nuts

3 eggs

50g caster sugar

150ml whole milk

150ml double cream

3tbsp dark rum

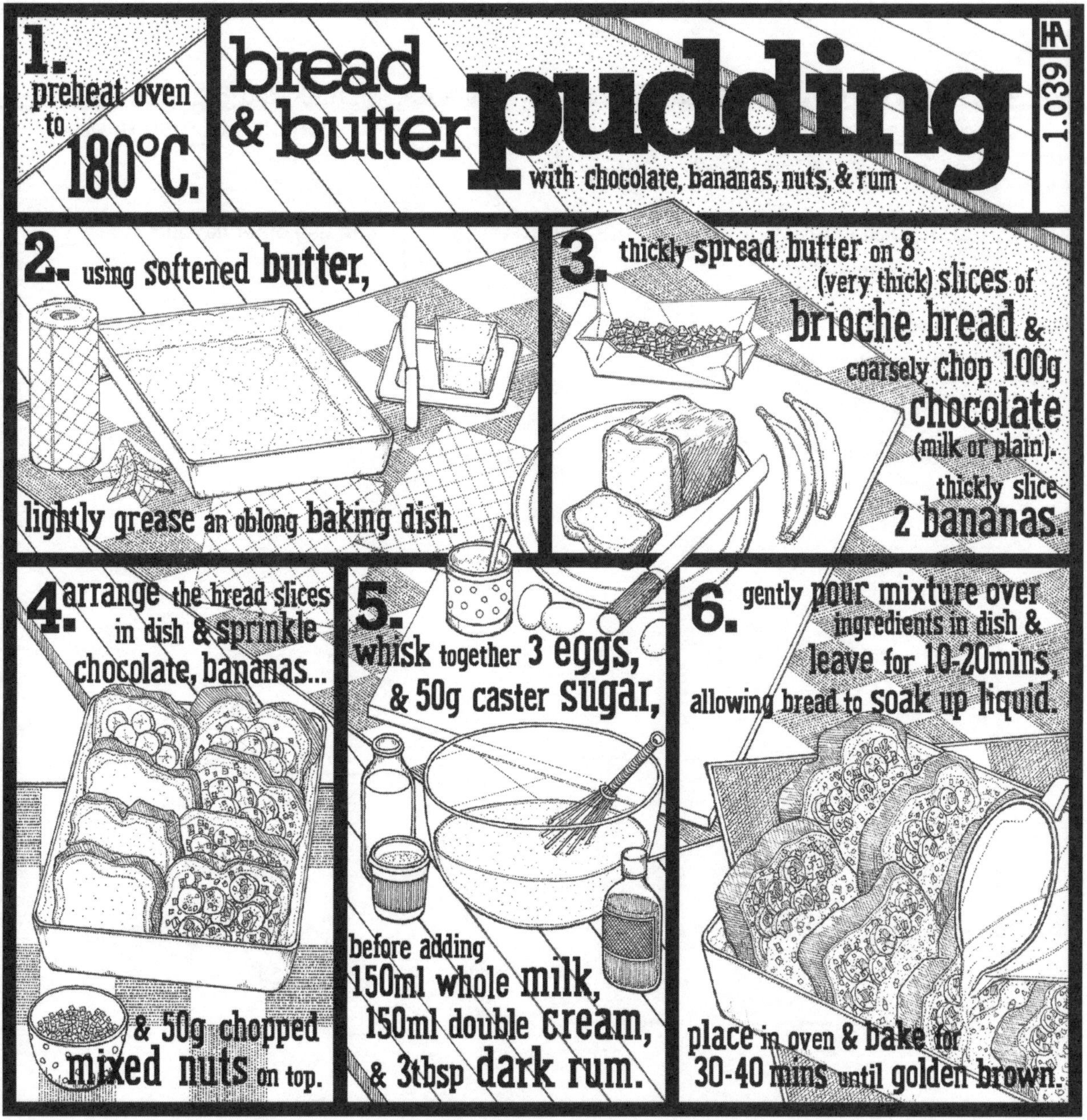
HA
1.039
bread & butter pudding
with chocolate, bananas, nuts, & rum
1. preheat oven to 180°C.
2. using softened butter,
lightly grease an oblong baking dish.
3. thickly spread butter on 8 (very thick) slices of brioche bread & coarsely chop 100g chocolate (milk or plain).
thickly slice 2 bananas.
4. arrange the bread slices in dish & sprinkle chocolate, bananas...
& 50g chopped mixed nuts on top.
5. whisk together 3 eggs, & 50g caster sugar,
before adding 150ml whole milk, 150ml double cream, & 3tbsp dark rum.
6. gently pour mixture over ingredients in dish & leave for 10-20mins, allowing bread to soak up liquid.
place in oven & bake for 30-40 mins until golden brown.

chocolate soufflé

makes 6-8 depending on size of dish used

- 200g orange-flavoured dark chocolate
- 150g butter
- 6 eggs
- 175g caster sugar
- 125g plain flour
- butter (for greasing dishes)

can use other flavours of chocolate.

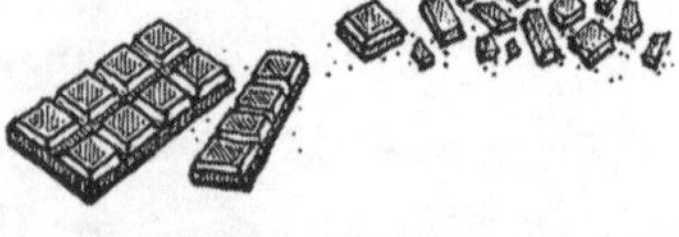

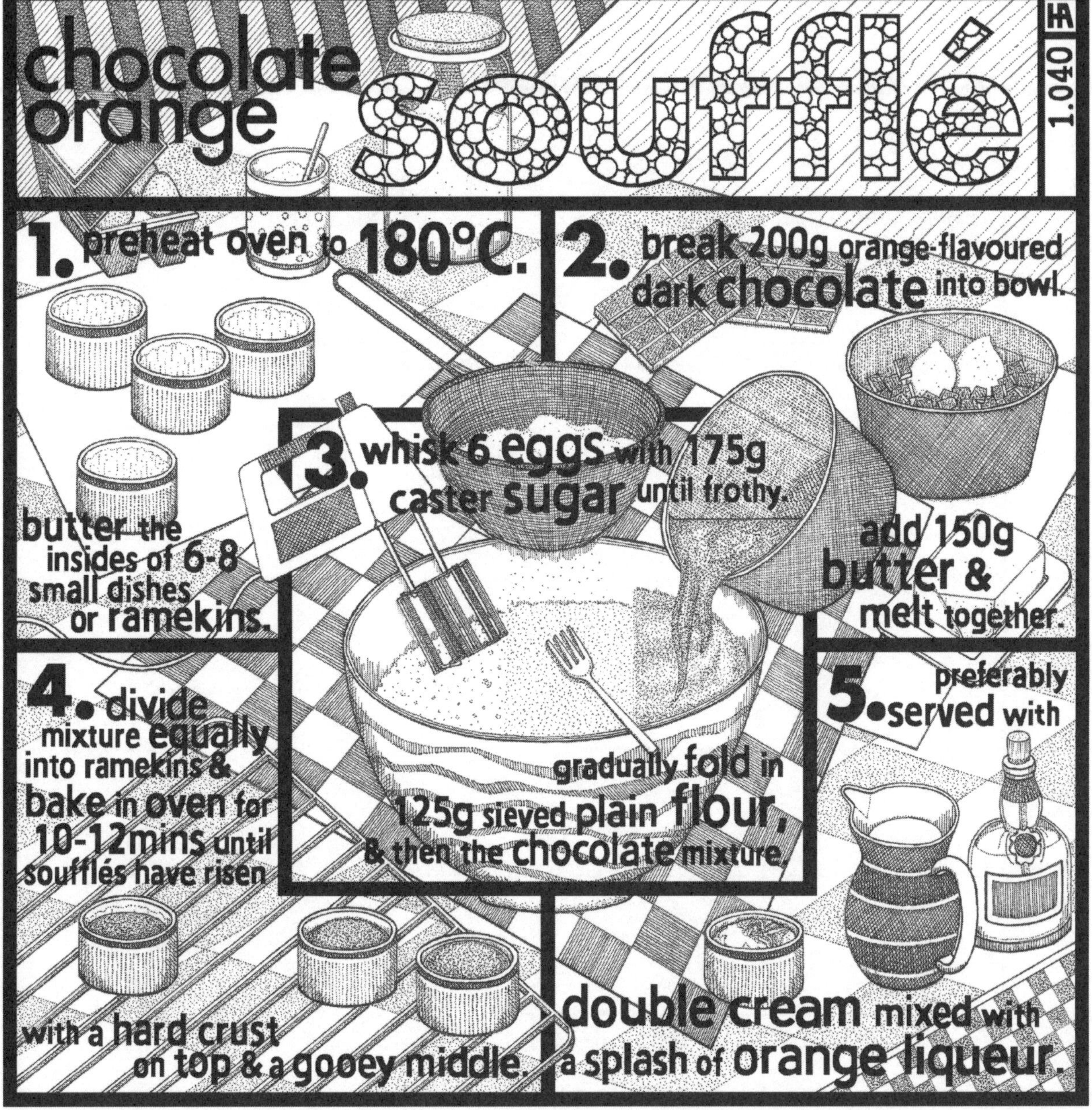
chocolate orange
soufflé
1.040
1. preheat oven to 180°C.
butter the insides of 6-8 small dishes or ramekins.
2. break 200g orange-flavoured dark chocolate into bowl.
add 150g butter & melt together.
3. whisk 6 eggs with 175g caster sugar until frothy.
gradually fold in 125g sieved plain flour, & then the chocolate mixture.
4. divide mixture equally into ramekins & bake in oven for 10-12mins until soufflés have risen
with a hard crust on top & a gooey middle.
5. preferably served with
double cream mixed with a splash of orange liqueur.

crème anglaise

serves 4

568ml whole milk
1 vanilla pod
4 egg yolks
225g caster sugar

ideally made to accompany *île flottante*.

could also be used as a substitute for custard.

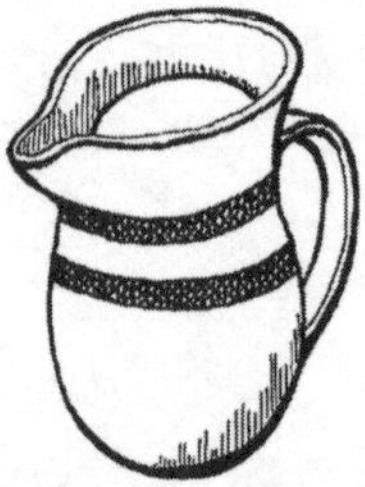

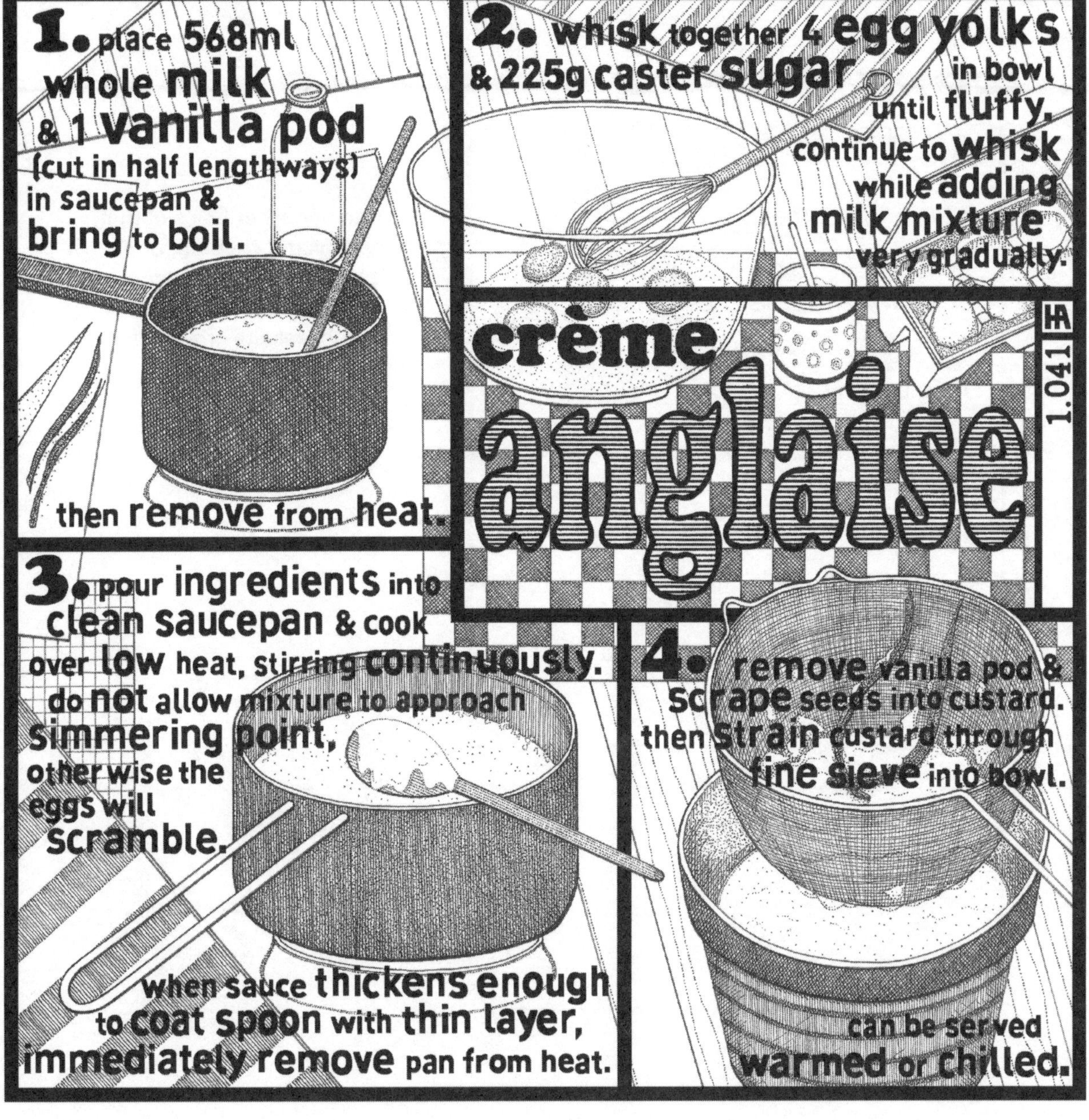
crème anglaise
1.041
1. place 568ml whole milk & 1 vanilla pod (cut in half lengthways) in saucepan & bring to boil.
then remove from heat.
2. whisk together 4 egg yolks & 225g caster sugar in bowl until fluffy.
continue to whisk while adding milk mixture very gradually.
3. pour ingredients into clean saucepan & cook over low heat, stirring continuously.
do not allow mixture to approach simmering point, otherwise the eggs will scramble.
when sauce thickens enough to coat spoon with thin layer, immediately remove pan from heat.
4. remove vanilla pod & scrape seeds into custard.
then strain custard through fine sieve into bowl.
can be served warmed or chilled.

gooseberry crumble

serves 4-6

700g gooseberries

2tbsp soft brown sugar (for fruit)

225g wholemeal self-raising flour

55g soft brown sugar (for crumble)

115g pecan nuts

115g butter

can use other types of fruit, e.g. plums, rhubarb, or blackberries, and different types of nuts in crumble, e.g. hazelnuts or walnuts.

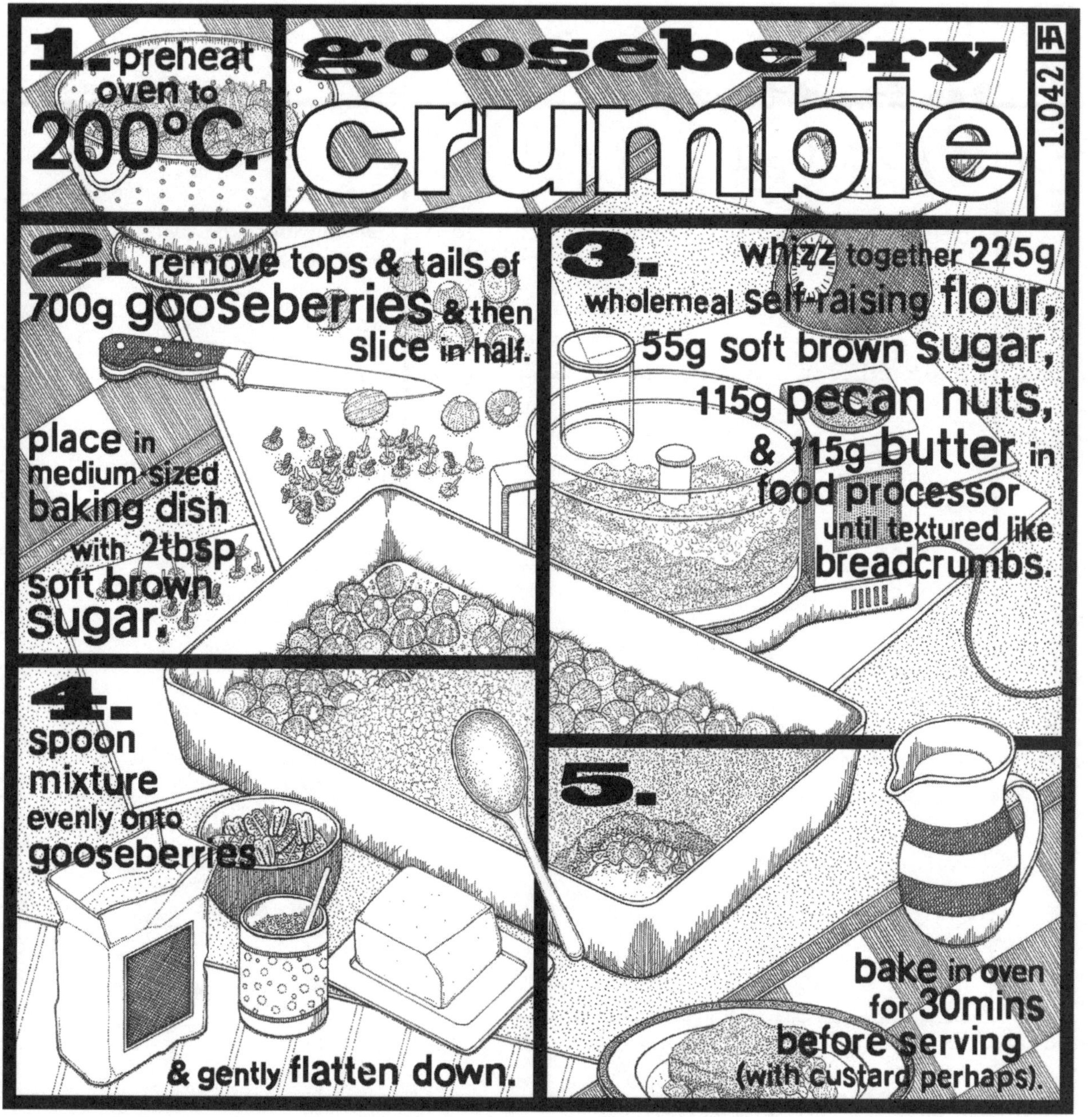

gooseberry
crumble
1.042
1. preheat oven to 200°C.
2. remove tops & tails of 700g gooseberries & then slice in half.
place in medium-sized baking dish with 2tbsp soft brown sugar.
3. whizz together 225g wholemeal self-raising flour, 55g soft brown sugar, 115g pecan nuts, & 115g butter in food processor until textured like breadcrumbs.
4. spoon mixture evenly onto gooseberries
& gently flatten down.
5.
bake in oven for 30mins before serving (with custard perhaps).

île flottante

makes 5-6

568ml whole milk
4 egg whites
1 pinch of salt
85g caster sugar

serve with *crème anglaise* and slivered almonds.

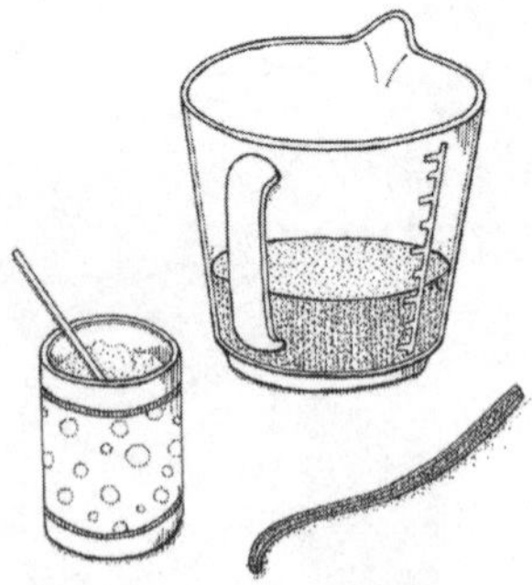

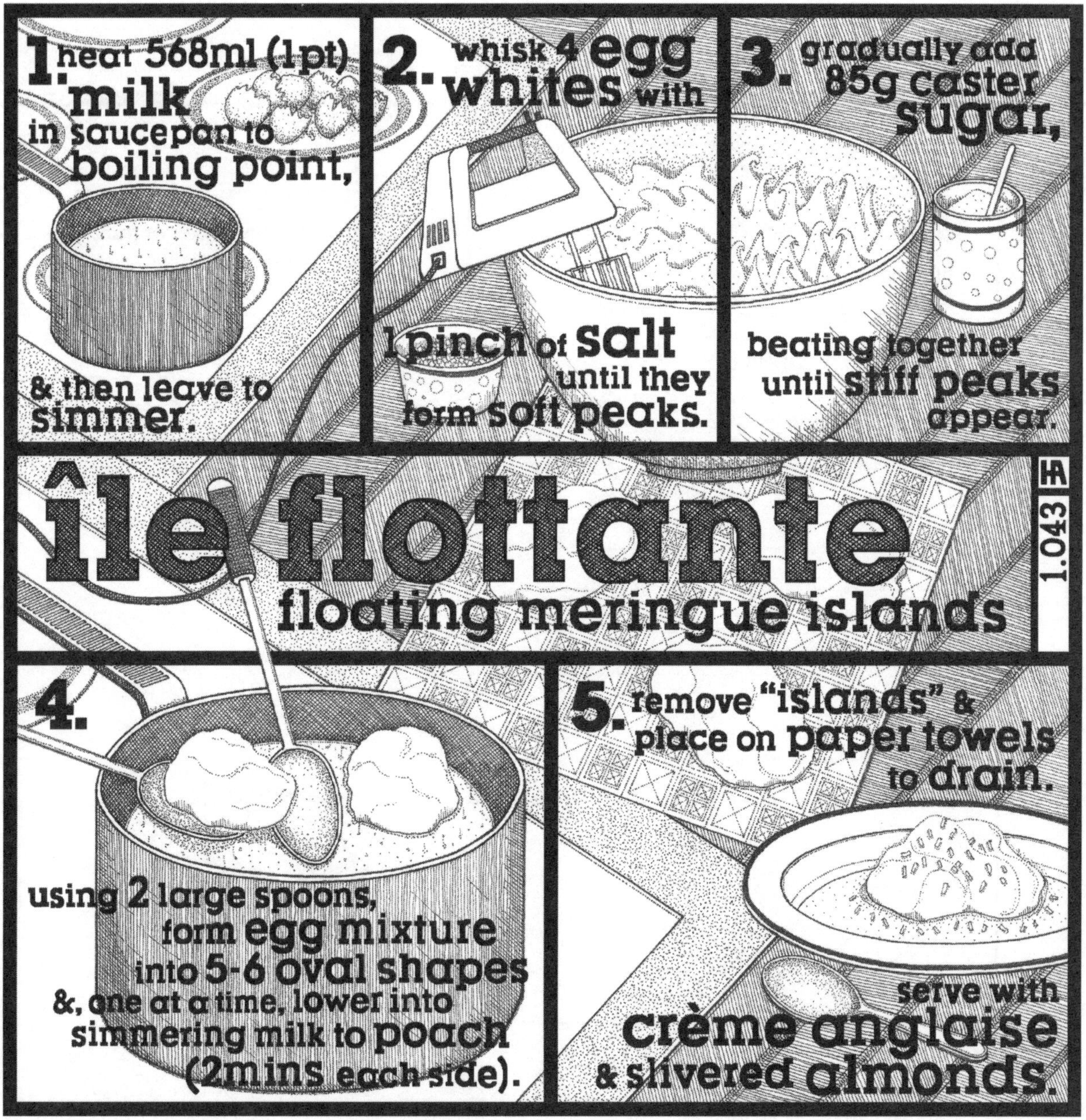
1. heat 568ml (1pt) milk in saucepan to boiling point,
& then leave to simmer.
2. whisk 4 egg whites with
1 pinch of salt until they form soft peaks.
3. gradually add 85g caster sugar,
beating together until stiff peaks appear.
île flottante
floating meringue islands
1.043
4.
using 2 large spoons, form egg mixture into 5-6 oval shapes &, one at a time, lower into simmering milk to poach (2mins each side).
5. remove "islands" & place on paper towels to drain.
serve with crème anglaise & slivered almonds.

rhubarb fool

serves 4

- 500g rhubarb stalks
- 150g caster sugar
- 300ml double cream
- seeds from 1 vanilla pod

can use other types of fruit, e.g. raspberries, gooseberries, etc.

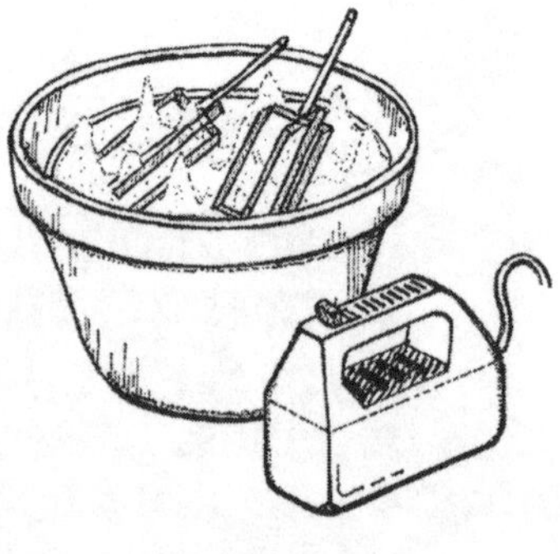

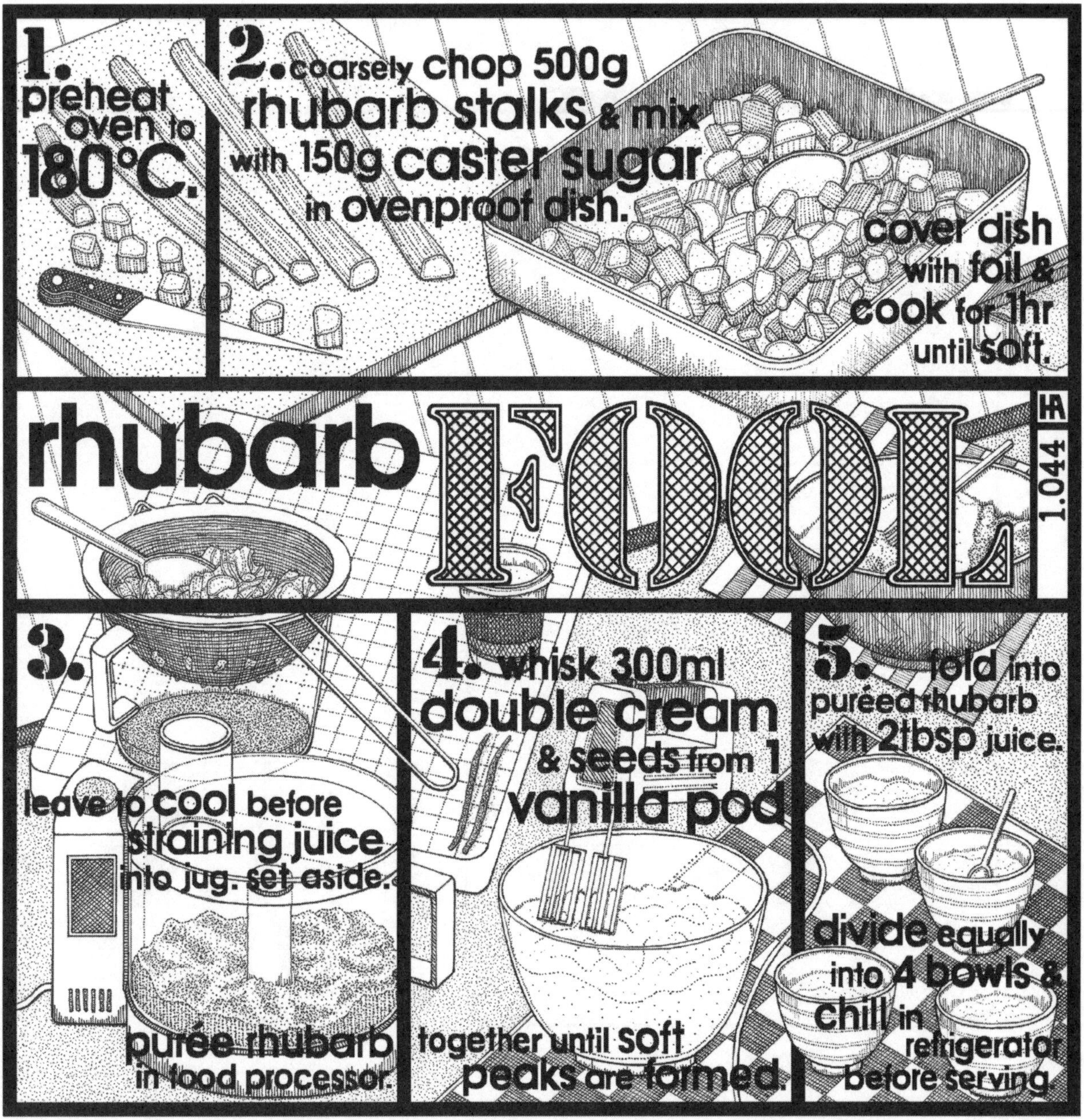
1. preheat oven to 180°C.
2. coarsely chop 500g rhubarb stalks & mix with 150g caster sugar in ovenproof dish.
cover dish with foil & cook for 1hr until soft.
rhubarb FOOL
HA
1.044
3.
leave to cool before straining juice into jug. set aside.
purée rhubarb in food processor.
4. whisk 300ml double cream & seeds from 1 vanilla pod
together until soft peaks are formed.
5. fold into puréed rhubarb with 2tbsp juice.
divide equally into 4 bowls & chill in refrigerator before serving.

rice pudding

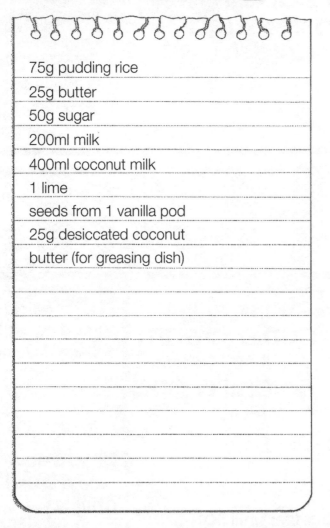

75g pudding rice

25g butter

50g sugar

200ml milk

400ml coconut milk

1 lime

seeds from 1 vanilla pod

25g desiccated coconut

butter (for greasing dish)

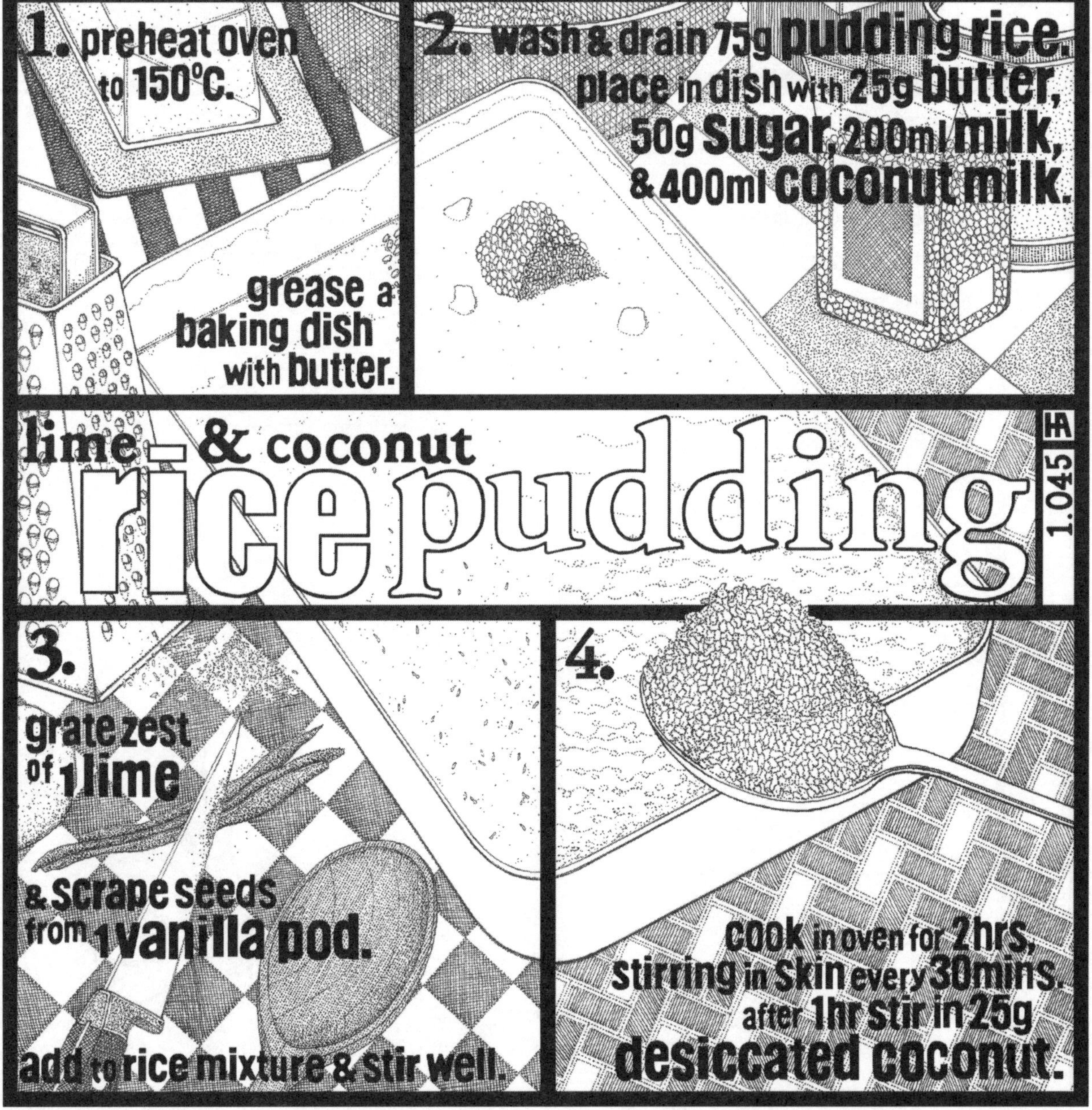
1. preheat oven to 150°C.
grease a baking dish with butter.
2. wash & drain 75g pudding rice. place in dish with 25g butter, 50g sugar, 200ml milk, & 400ml coconut milk.
lime & coconut rice pudding
HA 1.045
3. grate zest of 1 lime
& scrape seeds from 1 vanilla pod.
add to rice mixture & stir well.
4. cook in oven for 2hrs, stirring in skin every 30mins. after 1hr stir in 25g desiccated coconut.

Syllabub

serves 4

- zest & juice of 1 lime
- 3 lumps of preserved stem ginger (from jar)
- 2tbsp ginger syrup (from jar)
- 50ml white wine
- 50g caster sugar
- 300ml double cream

can be made with lemons or oranges instead of lime & ginger.

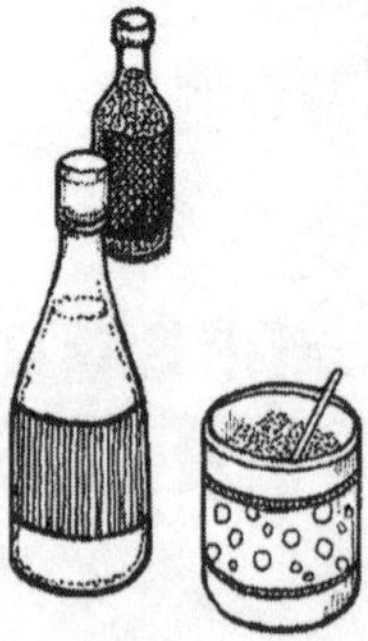

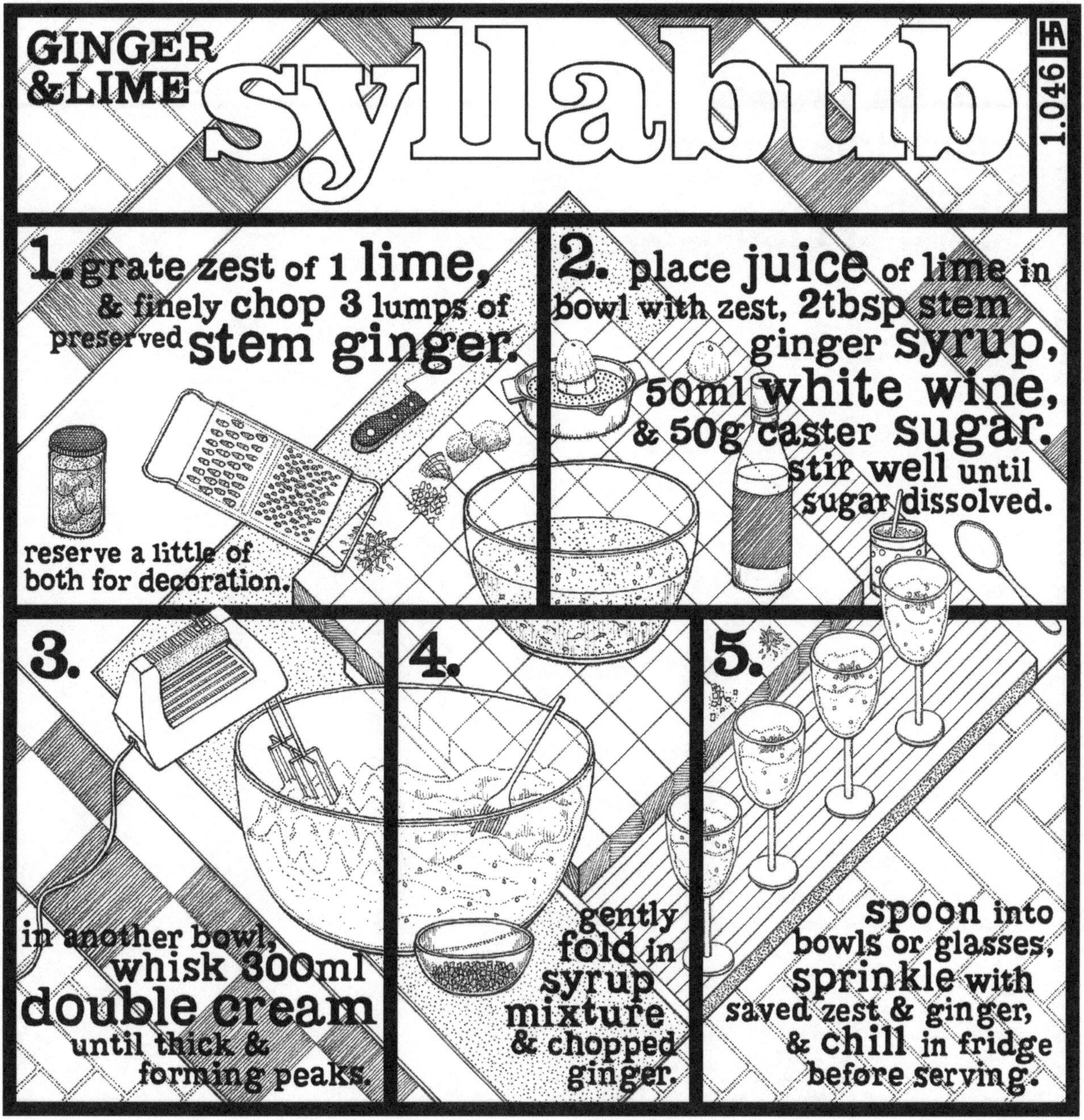
GINGER &LIME
syllabub
HA
1.046
1. grate zest of 1 lime, & finely chop 3 lumps of preserved stem ginger.
reserve a little of both for decoration.
2. place juice of lime in bowl with zest, 2tbsp stem ginger syrup, 50ml white wine, & 50g caster sugar.
stir well until sugar dissolved.
3.
in another bowl, whisk 300ml double cream until thick & forming peaks.
4.
gently fold in syrup mixture & chopped ginger.
5.
spoon into bowls or glasses, sprinkle with saved zest & ginger, & chill in fridge before serving.

cheese straws
chocolate brownies
flapjack
oatmeal & raisin cookies
scones
soda bread

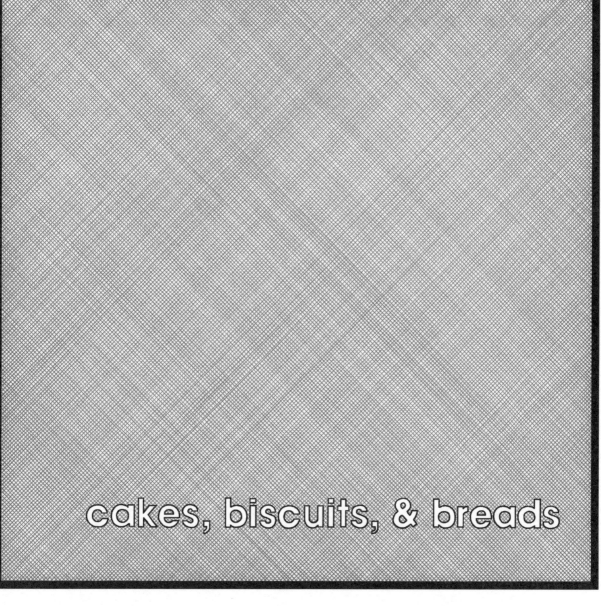

cakes, biscuits, & breads

cheese straws

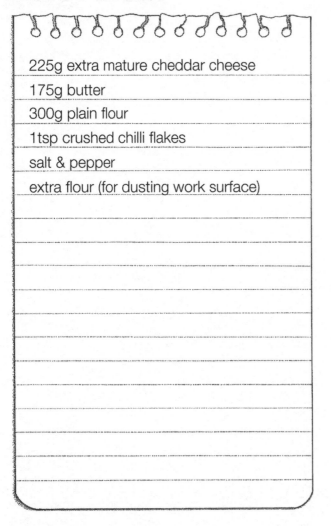

225g extra mature cheddar cheese

175g butter

300g plain flour

1tsp crushed chilli flakes

salt & pepper

extra flour (for dusting work surface)

can be made without
the crushed chilli flakes
for a less spicy version.

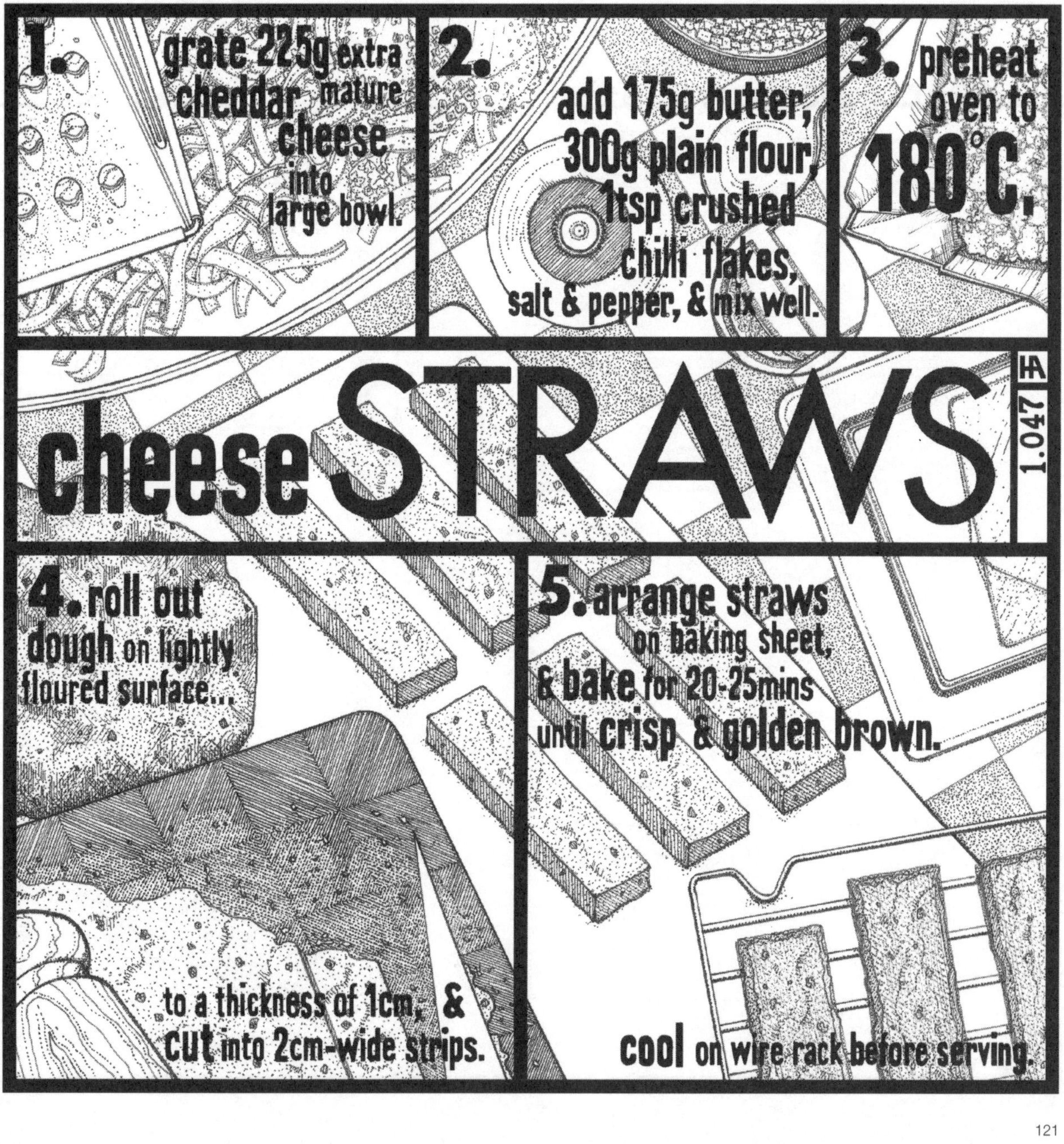

1. grate 225g extra mature cheddar cheese into large bowl.
2. add 175g butter, 300g plain flour, 1tsp crushed chilli flakes, salt & pepper, & mix well.
3. preheat oven to 180°C.
cheese STRAWS
1.047
4. roll out dough on lightly floured surface...
to a thickness of 1cm, & cut into 2cm-wide strips.
5. arrange straws on baking sheet, & bake for 20-25mins until crisp & golden brown.
cool on wire rack before serving.

chocolate brownies

makes 16-20

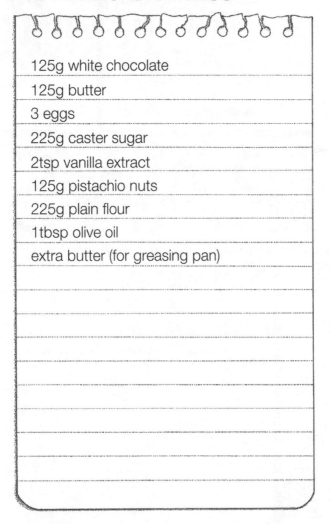

125g white chocolate

125g butter

3 eggs

225g caster sugar

2tsp vanilla extract

125g pistachio nuts

225g plain flour

1tbsp olive oil

extra butter (for greasing pan)

can be made with plain or milk chocolate, and different types of nuts.

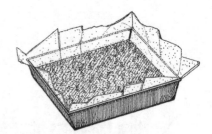

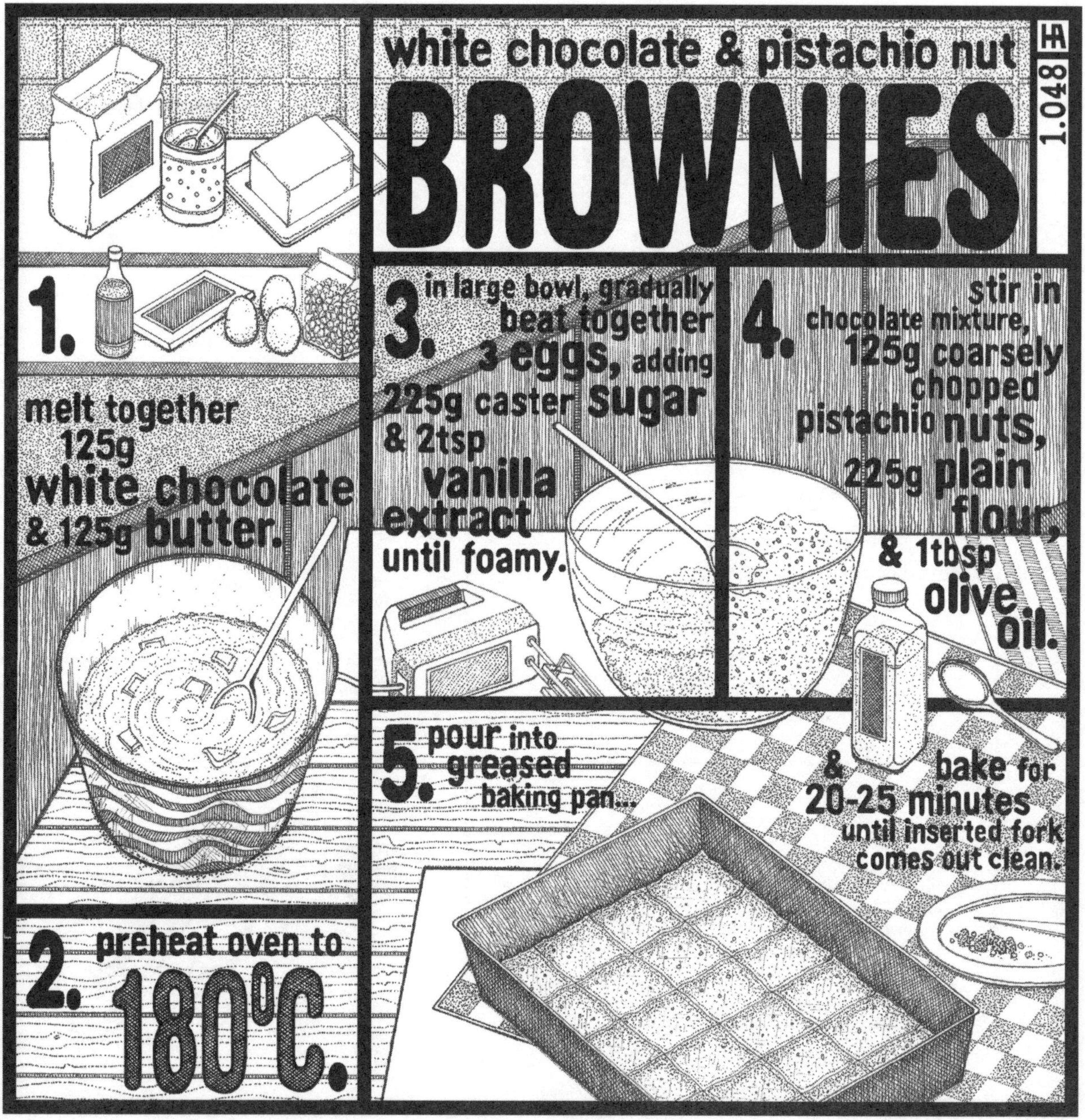
white chocolate & pistachio nut
BROWNIES
1.048
1.
melt together 125g white chocolate & 125g butter.
2. preheat oven to 180°C.
3. in large bowl, gradually beat together 3 eggs, adding 225g caster sugar & 2tsp vanilla extract until foamy.
4. stir in chocolate mixture, 125g coarsely chopped pistachio nuts, 225g plain flour, & 1tbsp olive oil.
5. pour into greased baking pan...
& bake for 20-25 minutes until inserted fork comes out clean.

flapjack

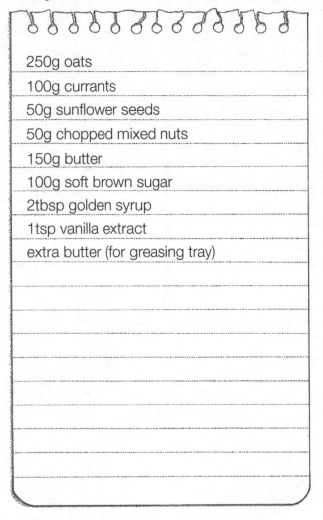

250g oats

100g currants

50g sunflower seeds

50g chopped mixed nuts

150g butter

100g soft brown sugar

2tbsp golden syrup

1tsp vanilla extract

extra butter (for greasing tray)

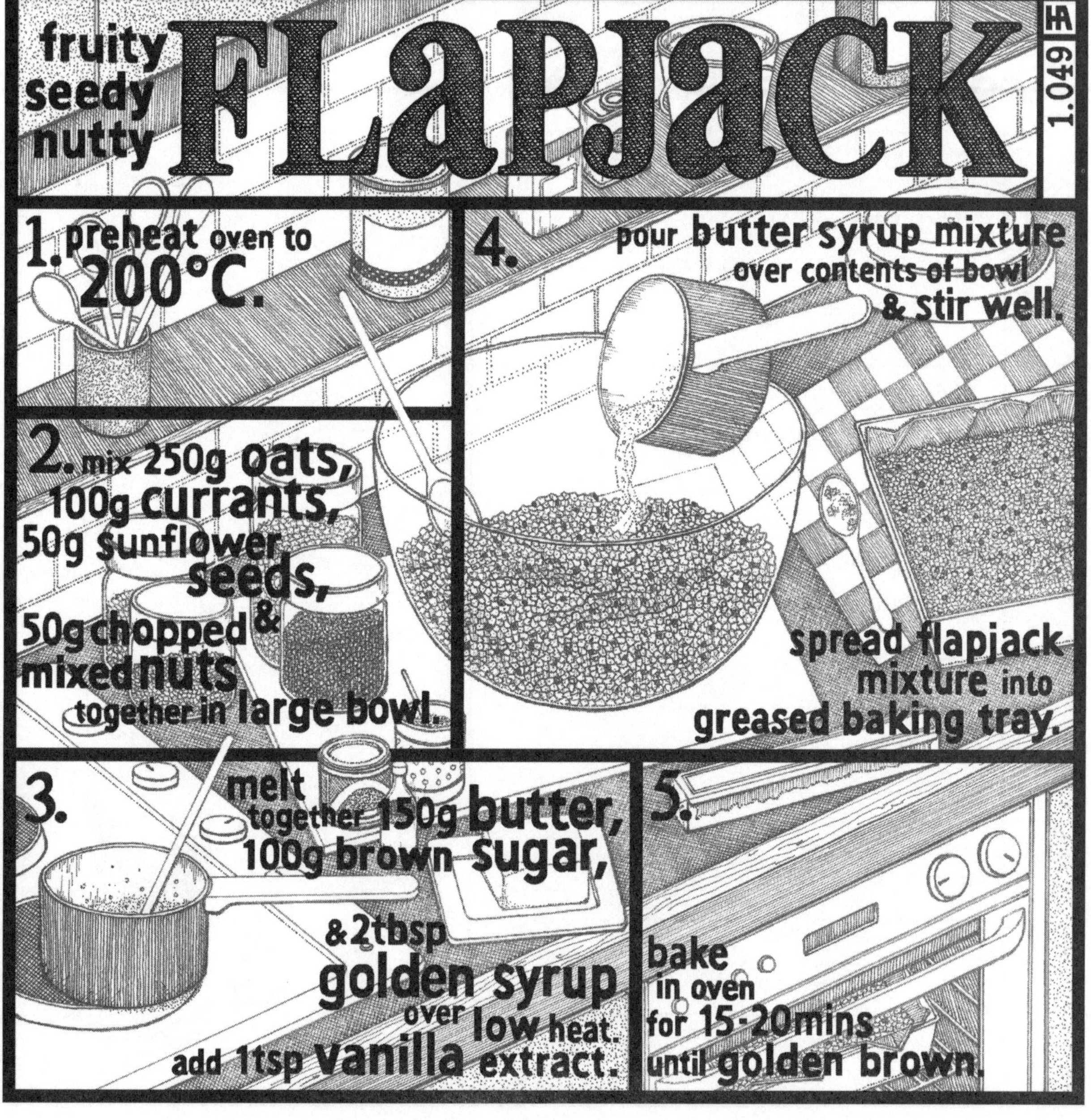
fruity
seedy
nutty
FLAPJACK
1.049
1. preheat oven to
200°C.
2. mix 250g oats,
100g currants,
50g sunflower seeds,
&
50g chopped mixed nuts
together in large bowl.
3. melt together 150g butter,
100g brown sugar,
&2tbsp
golden syrup
over low heat.
add 1tsp vanilla extract.
4. pour butter syrup mixture
over contents of bowl
& stir well.
spread flapjack
mixture into
greased baking tray.
5.
bake
in oven
for 15-20mins
until golden brown.

oatmeal & raisin cookies

makes 20

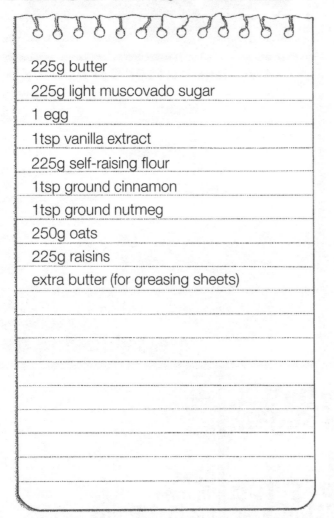

225g butter

225g light muscovado sugar

1 egg

1tsp vanilla extract

225g self-raising flour

1tsp ground cinnamon

1tsp ground nutmeg

250g oats

225g raisins

extra butter (for greasing sheets)

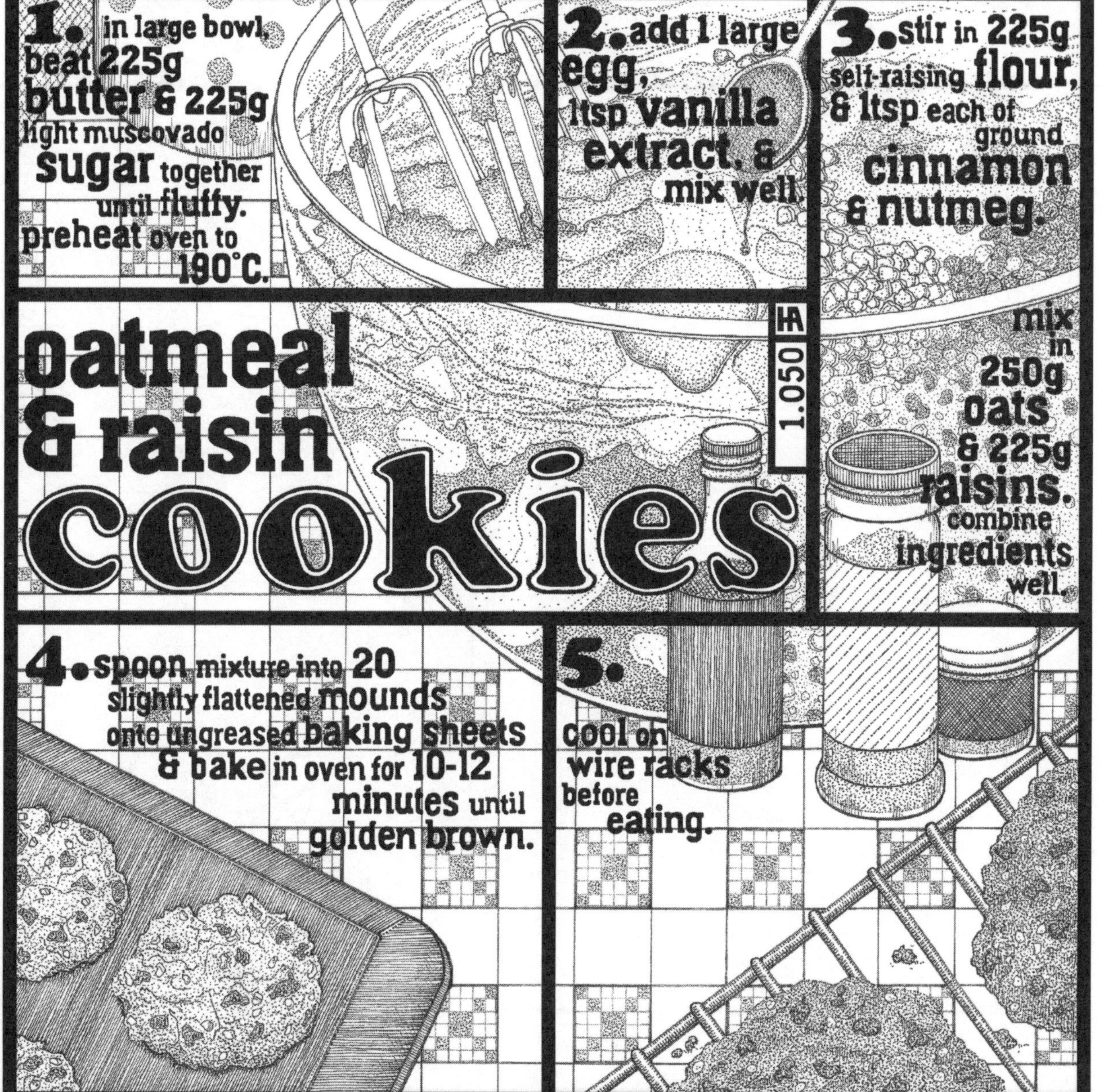
oatmeal
& raisin
cookies
HA
1.050
1. in large bowl, beat 225g butter & 225g light muscovado sugar together until fluffy. preheat oven to 190°C.
2. add 1 large egg, 1tsp vanilla extract, & mix well.
3. stir in 225g self-raising flour, & 1tsp each of ground cinnamon & nutmeg.
mix in 250g oats & 225g raisins. combine ingredients well.
4. spoon mixture into 20 slightly flattened mounds onto ungreased baking sheets & bake in oven for 10-12 minutes until golden brown.
5. cool on wire racks before eating.

apple & cinnamon **scones**

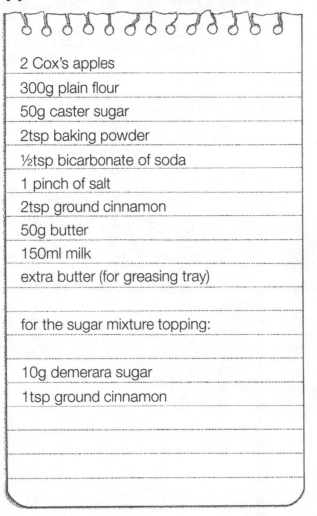

2 Cox's apples

300g plain flour

50g caster sugar

2tsp baking powder

½tsp bicarbonate of soda

1 pinch of salt

2tsp ground cinnamon

50g butter

150ml milk

extra butter (for greasing tray)

for the sugar mixture topping:

10g demerara sugar

1tsp ground cinnamon

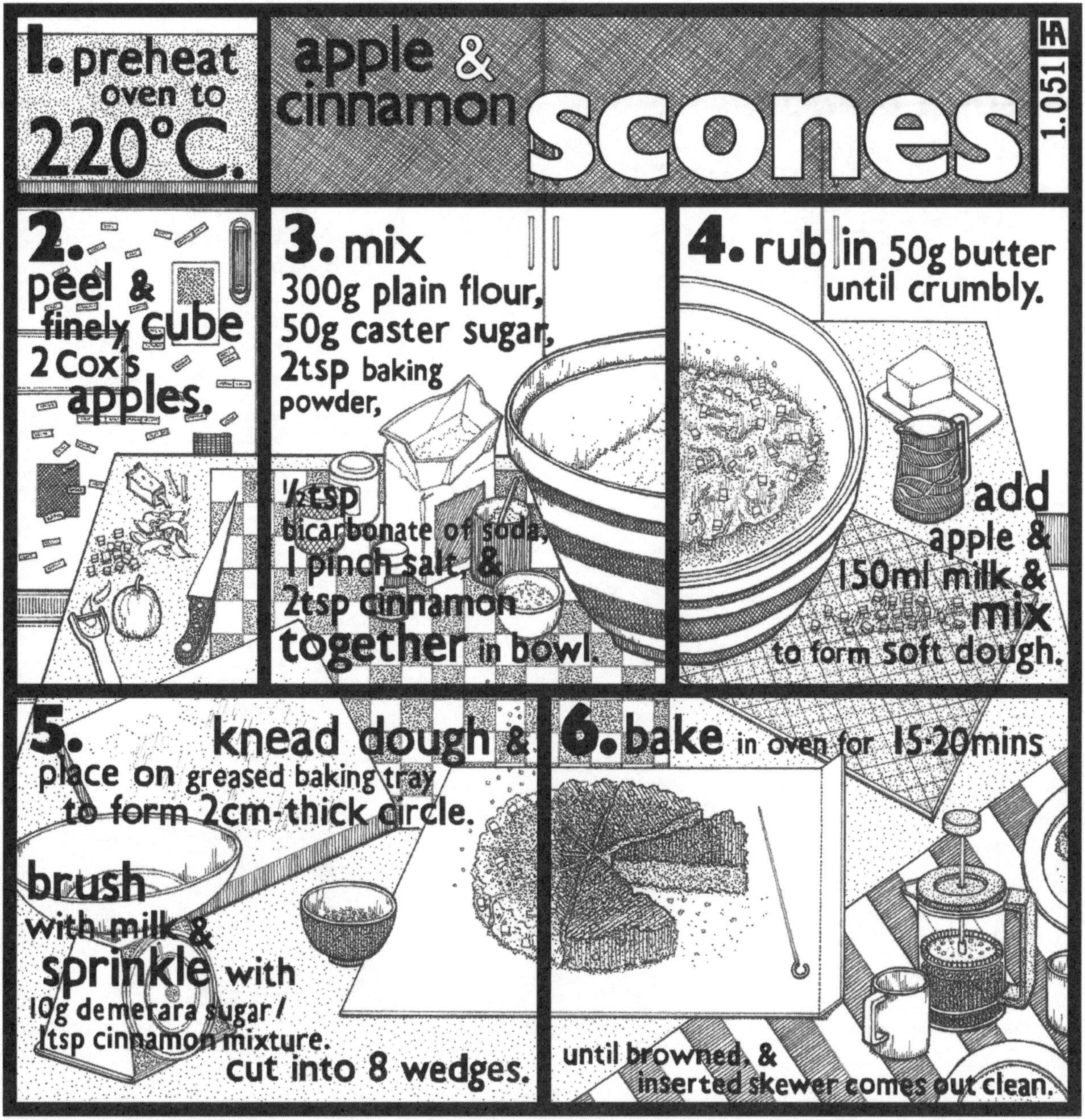
1. preheat oven to 220°C.
apple & cinnamon scones
1.051
2. peel & finely cube 2 Cox's apples.
3. mix 300g plain flour, 50g caster sugar, 2tsp baking powder,
½tsp bicarbonate of soda, 1 pinch salt, & 2tsp cinnamon together in bowl.
4. rub in 50g butter until crumbly.
add apple & 150ml milk & mix to form soft dough.
5. knead dough & place on greased baking tray to form 2cm-thick circle.
brush with milk & sprinkle with 10g demerara sugar/1tsp cinnamon mixture.
cut into 8 wedges.
6. bake in oven for 15-20mins
until browned. & inserted skewer comes out clean.

soda bread

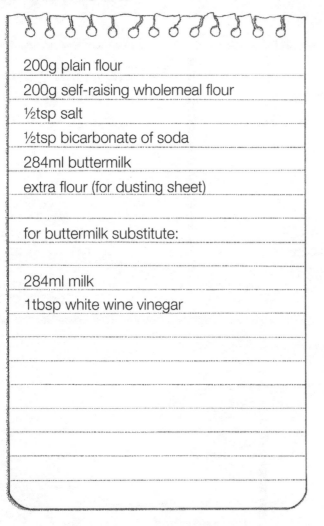

200g plain flour

200g self-raising wholemeal flour

½tsp salt

½tsp bicarbonate of soda

284ml buttermilk

extra flour (for dusting sheet)

for buttermilk substitute:

284ml milk

1tbsp white wine vinegar

can add 100g raisins or 100g walnuts.

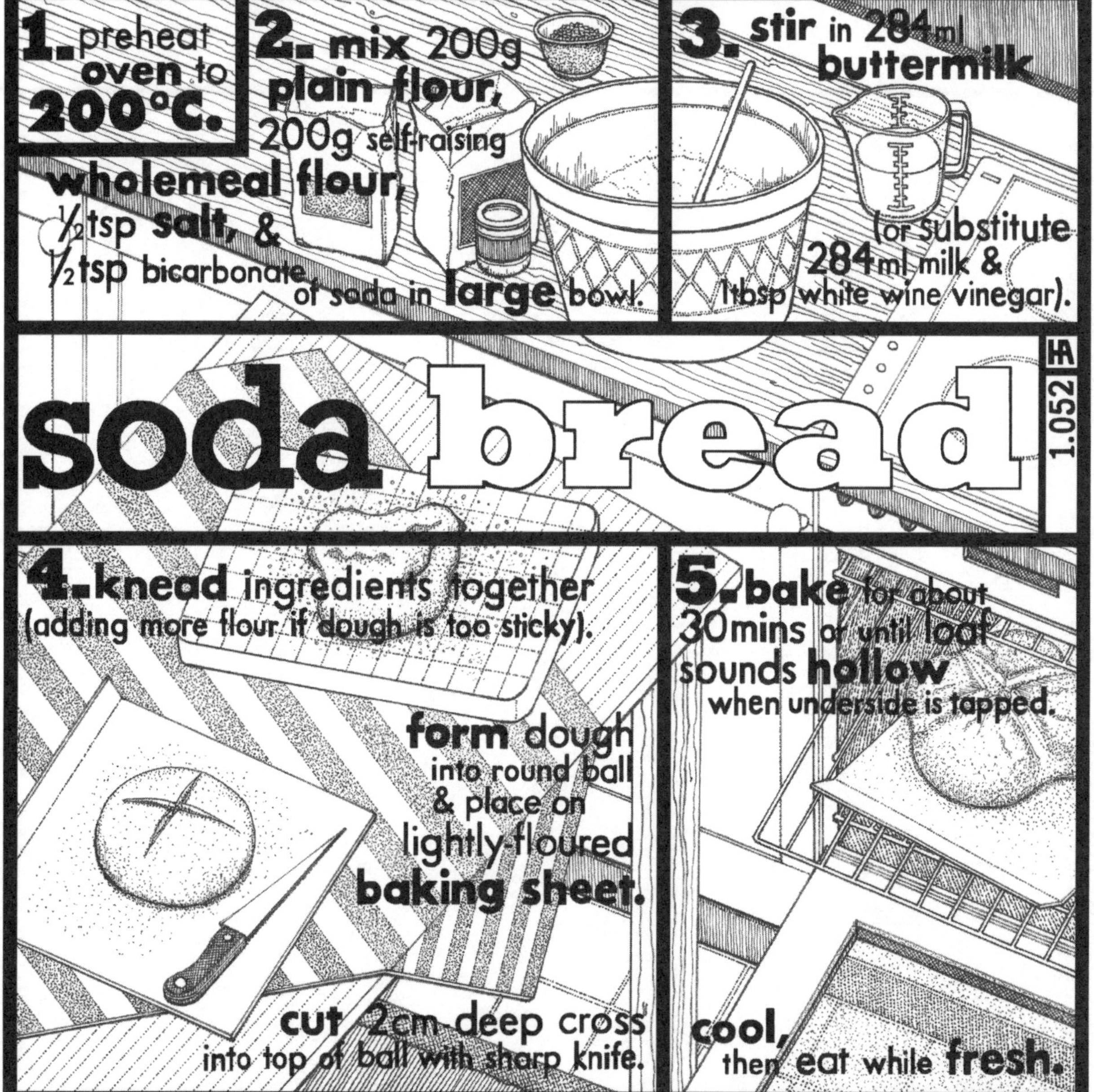
1. preheat oven to 200°C.
2. mix 200g plain flour, 200g self-raising wholemeal flour, ½tsp salt, & ½tsp bicarbonate of soda in large bowl.
3. stir in 284ml buttermilk
(or substitute 284ml milk & 1tbsp white wine vinegar).
soda bread
1.052
4. knead ingredients together (adding more flour if dough is too sticky).
form dough into round ball & place on lightly-floured baking sheet.
cut 2cm-deep cross into top of ball with sharp knife.
5. bake for about 30mins or until loaf sounds hollow when underside is tapped.
cool, then eat while fresh.

acknowledgements

I would like to thank all those who have helped in the making of this book, and in particular:

The recipients of my original twelve-part magnetic Comic Book Cook Book, including: Storm and Stephen; Ed and Joan; James, Nik, Louis and Ewan; John and Sue W; Rachel S; John C; Andrew; Linda; Wendy; Frances C N; Frank and Jessica D; and my godfather, John C N.

For friendship, support and inspiration: the tasters of Gorse Lane, including Glen and Alison, Aris and Ibalia, and Vivienne and David; the Hotel Boxville posse; the Collier household, including Jacob and Ethan; my godson, Theo; Felix; Dylan; Cookie; Stephen Cranham; Jo, and her checkerboard tiles; Rupert; Charlie; the 33MT crew, including Storm U and Spikel A; absent friends, and my parents.

For professional advice and assistance: my editors, Rowan Yapp and Caroline McArthur; my agent, Antony Topping, at Greene and Heaton; and Frances Macmillan.

Rachael: for providing me with shelter from the storm, and being a most wonderful friend.

MJ: for her proofreading, indefatigable encouragement, unflagging moral support, and invaluable friendship.

And finally, my brother, Tommy: for his proofreading too, but also for his all-round brilliance, his sense of beauty, and without whom this book would most probably be nothing.

For further information about Recipes From the Kitchen Drawer and related merchandise, please go to www.kitchendrawerrecipes.com.

Index

A

B

C

E

F

G

H

I

J

K

L

M

N

O

P

Q
R

S

T

U
V

W
X
Y
Z

Published by Square Peg 2012

1 3 5 7 9 8 6 4 2

First published in Great Britain in 2012 by
SQUARE PEG
Random House, 20 Vauxhall Bridge Road,
London SW1V 2SA

www.randomhouse.co.uk

Addresses for companies within The Random House Group Limited can be found at:
www.randomhouse.co.uk/offices.htm

The Random House Group Limited Reg. No. 954009

A CIP catalogue record for this book is available from the British Library

ISBN 978 0 22 408703 2

The Random House Group Limited supports The Forest Stewardship Council (FSC ®),
the leading international forest certification organisation. Our books carrying the FSC
label are printed on FSC ® certified paper. FSC is the only forest certification scheme
endorsed by the leading environmental organisations, including Greenpeace. Our
paper procurement policy can be found at www.randomhouse.co.uk/environment

Printed and bound in Great Britain by MPG Books Ltd, Bodmin, Cornwall

FSC